When Life Gets Rough

When Life Gets Rough

Tips for Coping with 13 of Life's Traumas

Though this book is designed for group study, it
is also intended for your personal enjoyment and
spiritual growth. A leader's guide is available from
your local bookstore or from your publisher.

Copyright 1986

Beacon Hill Press of Kansas City
Kansas City, Missouri

Printed in the United States of America

Stephen M. Miller
Editor

Mary Jo Van Dyne
Editorial Assistant

Editorial Committee
Jack Mottweiler, *Chairman*
David Holdren
Stephen M. Miller
Carl Pierce
Gene Van Note
Lyle Williams

Photo and Art Credits

Cover, Comstock; 1, Universal Press Syndicate, 4400 Johnson Dr., Fairway, KS 66205; 8, 36, 57, Bob Taylor; 16, Bo Brown; 24, 51, reprinted with permission of *The Saturday Evening Post Society,* a division of BFL & MS, Inc. © 1984, 1985; 43, Jim Whitmer; 63, Betty Woods; 69, Creative Media Services, Box 5955, Berkeley, CA 94705; 76, H. Armstrong Roberts; 85, Jonathan A. Meyers; 92, Master's Agency; 103, Vernon Sigl.

The following versions of Scripture have been used by permission:

All Bible quotations are taken from *The Holy Bible, New International Version* (NIV), unless otherwise noted. Copyright © 1973, 1978, 1984 by International Bible Society.

The Living Bible (TLB), © 1971 by Tyndale House Publishers, Wheaton, Ill.

The New Testament in Modern English (Phillips), Revised Edition © J. B. Phillips 1958, 1960, 1972. By permission of the MacMillan Publishing Co.

The *New English Bible* (NEB), © The Delegates of the Oxford University Press and The Syndics of the Cambridge University Press, 1961, 1970.

ISBN 083-411-1160

10   9   8   7

OTHER DIALOG SERIES TITLES

Christians at Work in a Hurting World

Christians in a Crooked World

Clean Living in a Dirty World

Coping with Traumas of Family Life

Dear God . . . Help Me Understand

Growing Season: Maturing of a Christian

How to Improve Your Prayer Life

How to Live the Holy Life

I Believe: Now Tell Me Why

Less Stress, Please

Misguiding Lights? The Gospel According to . . .

No Easy Answers: Christians Debate Today's Issues

Questions You Shouldn't Ask About Christianity

Questions You Shouldn't Ask About the Church

Raising Kids

Spiritual Zest: Finding It and Keeping It

The Me I See: A Christian Approach to Self-Esteem

Turning Points . . . That Can Make Us or Break Us

What Jesus Said About . . .

For a description of all available Dialog Series books, including some that may not be listed here, ask for a free brochure from your favorite Christian bookstore, your denominational distributor, or Beacon Hill Press of Kansas City.

Contents

Chapter 1   **When Your Friends Let You Down**   7
Stephen M. Miller

Chapter 2   **The Trauma of Moving**   15
C. Ellen Watts

Chapter 3   **Out of a Job . . . or About to Be**   23
James C. Hefley

Chapter 4   **Working Through Loneliness**   35
Larry Jones

Chapter 5   **A Parent's Shattered Dreams**   42
Guy Greenfield

Chapter 6   **When the Marriage Begins to Wither**   50
Jan Frye

Chapter 7   **When You Lose Your Health**   56
Kenneth E. Schemmer

Chapter 8   **Whatever Happened to Integrity?**   62
Bill Manning

Chapter 9   **Stress—a Christian Survival Kit**   68
Randall E. Davey

Chapter 10   **When You Lose Your Hope**   75
Robert Schuller

Chapter 11   **When Someone You Care About Does You Wrong**   84
David Augsburger

Chapter 12   **Coping with Old Age— Yours and Your Parents'**   91
Nina Beegle

Chapter 13   **Death: The Longest Good-bye**   102
Becky Smith

Chapter 1

When Your Friends Let You Down

by Stephen M. Miller

Background Scripture: Psalm 55:12-14; Romans 14:19; 15:7

MY MOM and I were accused of soliciting black market quiz questions of the Bible. Can you believe it?

I was a teenager on our church's Bible quiz team, at the time. The team had done quite well in competition that year. And at the end of the regular season, three of us were invited to compete in a multistate contest to see who would represent our region at the coming international quizzes.

To help us review for this competition, our quiz director promised to give the three of us copies of all the questions she had drilled us on during the season. I still don't know why she gave big stacks of study questions to my teammates, and only a few sheets of random questions to me. Had this been a time when photocopiers were popular, I probably would have gotten my share. But it wasn't, and I didn't.

I was afraid to confront the quiz director about this. But my mom wasn't.

And when the fragile-egoed director suddenly found herself put on the spot, she blasted off and became a missile on the hunt.

To Mom, she denied the charge of unfairness. To the rest of the church, she spread the story that Mom and I had asked her for a copy of the actual questions that would be used at the regional competition—black market quiz questions.

The next couple of months were a nightmare. When I went to church—and I wouldn't have gone had my folks not down-right insisted—I might as well have been wearing a sign that read: UNCLEAN. My friends hardly spoke to me. Here I was bleeding to death emotionally, and they were doing little more than spitting an occasional "Hi, how are ya" at me. I needed a

kind word and a sympathetic ear. But all I got were cheap greetings and no ears at all.

It hurts when our friends let us down like this. And there are a lot of ways friends can disappoint us. I think this true story I just told represents one of the most common ways friends let us down. We get hurt, we need help and encouragement, and the best our friends can come up with is silence and elbow room. We're falsely accused, newly divorced, traumatized by a son who gets arrested for doing dope, and suddenly we're on our own. Our friends scatter.

But friends can disappoint us not only by keeping silent when they should be talking but also by yapping when they should be keeping quiet.

You tell your best friend a deep, dark secret, a confidential bit of news, or a frustration you're having with someone, then your friend goes and blabs it.

That not only makes us mad but also can get us in big trouble. I told a friend of mine about a problem I was having with a coworker, and my friend repeated the story to that coworker. Of course, that employee was quite insulted. So she complained to her supervisor that I was maligning her name. It took an office meeting to resolve that tense situation.

Another way our friends can let us down is by failing to defend us when we're attacked. When Jesus was arrested in the Garden of Gethsemane, I can't help but think he was just a little pleased when Peter sliced off that guard's ear. Even though Jesus rebuked the disciple, I think Christ must have smiled inside at Peter's willingness to protect his Friend.

Friends can also disappoint us by taking advantage of us. And I'm afraid this is all too common. I've seen backyard mechanics frustrated into near profanity with friends who drive up in clunkers at the most inconvenient time, expecting to get prompt service and a bill for only the parts.

And I've heard about the couple who figured out a way to get rid of their kids every Sunday afternoon. They coached their children to go up to a preselected friend of the family after the church service and say, "Can we go home with you today?"

Nearly every Sunday, this conniving couple was able to spend quiet afternoons together while their friends watched the kids.

And I know of a middle-aged couple out West who had to put up with a couple of supper moochers. The moochers were the wife's sister and her roommate. Every night, these two women came over for a visit—just before supper. The married couple were polite folks and always invited them to share in the meal—and the women always accepted, happily. Immediately after the meal was over, the moochers left.

Night after night, this continued. Eventually, the husband got fed up, so to speak. And he insisted that his wife confront her sister. But his wife couldn't muster up the courage. So the husband said he'd take care of the matter, if the wife would agree to play along. She agreed.

The next night, the two women arrived on time, bellies growling. And they ate supper, as usual. But as they prepared to leave, the husband invited them to stay for an extra cup of coffee and a little talk.

It was during this talk that he called in his big, ugly, dirty dog. The husband then lowered each plate, one-by-one, so the dog could lick it sparkling clean. The wife then took the plates, toweled them off, and put them in the cupboard.

9

After that, the married couple was never able to convince the moochers to share another meal. Of course, all the dishes were thoroughly scoured right after the moochers left. But nobody told them.

Now this isn't the best way to resolve the problem, especially if you cherish the friendship. But in a desperate situation, this is one desperate measure that would probably work.

Friends can also let us down by failing to spend as much time with us as we think they should. Our friends get busy with special projects, a new baby in the home, or new friends, and suddenly we feel left out and even rejected.

But probably the most devastating thing a friend can do to us is turn on us and attack. The Psalmist puts it so well. "It was not an enemy who taunted me—then I could have borne it; I could have hidden and escaped. But it was you, a man like myself, my companion and my friend. What fellowship we had, what wonderful discussion as we walked together to the Temple of the Lord on holy days" (Psalm 55:12-14, TLB).

How to Heal the Wound

When a friend lets you down, consider these eight suggestions before you call in the dog.

1. Face the problem. Admit that the situation is bothering you and that you can't ignore it any longer if the friendship is to survive.

2. Consider your friend's side of the issue. Try to understand why your friend did what he did, or didn't do what you think he should have done. Pray for insight.

When I was falsely accused of wanting those black market quiz questions, my friends knew I wasn't guilty. But they also correctly guessed this was a real emotional issue with me, and they didn't know what to say. That's a human response they had. And looking back on it, I can relate to it. I've struggled with how to respond to friends when they become engulfed in crises. But one thing I don't give them anymore is dead silence and a moonscape full of elbow room.

3. Plan to discuss the problem with your friend. Talk about it when you can have a quiet time together and when you're both in a good mood and well rested. Discuss your feelings honestly, but don't attack your friend—either in your selection of words or in the volume and tone of your voice. Keep your voice low. And stick to the issue at hand; don't pick the scabs off old wounds.

4. *Listen.* Try to hear and understand what your friend has to say. And if you sense your friend is not being completely open with you, say so. Encourage him to share, without bullying him into it.

5. *Cooperate with your friend.* Don't be the enemy. Be a friend who wants to get the issue out in the open so it can be resolved. You'll find your goal in Romans 14:19, "Make every effort to do what leads to peace and to mutual edification."

6. *Be prepared to disagree.* Sometimes, you will have one opinion, while your friend has the opposite. And usually that's OK. After all, there are two brains at work here, with two different sets of life experiences. Learn to enjoy the different perspective your friend has on things. Face it, if all your friends were just like you, you'd be in for one boring life. *Vive la différence.*

7. *Forgive and ask forgiveness.* Forgive your friend, silently if he doesn't think he did anything wrong. And ask forgiveness if you feel he thinks you were in the wrong. Maybe you were guilty of expecting too much of him.

8. *Affirm your love for your friend.* Make up with the gift of a warm handshake, a hug, or a dinner on you.

I earned money during part of my college days by working in a gas station. One day, an unsaved friend of mine lost his temper about something. I happened to be nearby, and he shoved me up against the wall.

There was no call for this, and he felt terrible about it later. But he was the kind of person who found it tough to say things like, "I'm sorry" or "I was wrong." But the next day, he had nothing but praise for me, and he helped me do some of the jobs that were traditionally mine. The message was clear. He was embarrassed and sorry. I responded with words of praise and appreciation, without referring to the angry moment of the day before. Once again, all was well. The wound was healed. The friendship grew even stronger. And he never shoved me again. (But that could be at least partly because I kept out of his way when he got mad.)

Nurturing the Friendship

Once the wound is mended, don't assume the friendship will blossom untended, like the Garden of Eden. You're going to have to work at it. And as you do, keep these suggestions in mind.

1. Give your friends the freedom to be themselves, to think and express their own thoughts, to pursue their own interests. Don't plow into them for supporting the Republican presidential candidate, or for accepting an invitation to share Sunday dinner with someone else on the one Sunday a month you normally eat together.

2. Accept your friends as they are, limitations and all. Don't expect them to be superhuman, and above weakness and failure. My friend, who repeated with embellishment my complaints about a coworker, is a friend who has a tough time keeping things to herself. She's working on this, but she still has a ways to go.

Did I dump her and say, "With friends like you, I sure don't need enemies"? Nope. I'm aware of her weakness, and I try to keep it in mind when I talk with her. But she is still a friend whose company I enjoy.

"Accept one another . . . just as Christ accepted you" (Romans 15:7).

3. Be honest with your friends. Express your feelings, good and bad, instead of imprisoning them in a pressure cooker.

Jennifer was a college student who made friends during the summer with a new girl in town, Terri. The two hit it off just right. The friendship chemistry was perfect. And since the two would be going to the same school, Jennifer thought this was going to be a lasting friendship.

But when school started, life moved into high gear. The once-frequent phone calls became sporadic as Terri developed new friendships and as Jennifer maintained her shallow acquaintances and drowned her loneliness in a hundred school activities.

Jennifer deeply missed the close friendship she had experienced with Terri. It had been real, and she wanted it to continue. But Terri seemed busy, and happy with her new friends.

Finally, Jennifer decided to find out one way or another if Terri still wanted the special friendship. She took a chance on being rejected.

"Terri," she said in a strained voice, "when we became friends last summer, it was one of the best things that ever happened to me. But now, with school and all, it seems as though our friendship is dying. We don't have time for each other anymore. I miss our close friendship, and I want it to continue. But if you don't want it, I need to know."

Terri put her hand on Jennifer's shoulder and said, "Oh, Jenny, I've noticed what's been happening, too. And I feel terrible. We grew so close this summer that I still consider you my best friend. Let's work on spending more time together."

Jennifer's honesty was not without risk, but it saved a great friendship.

4. *Learn to give and take.* This goes for encouragement, loyalty, praise, and hands-on help.

It's hard for some of us independent types to accept help from our friends, especially when we're swept up into a problem that doesn't sit well with some church folks: our daughter gets pregnant and plans to keep the baby, our son decides to marry a girl of another race, our spouse walks out on us.

Too many times, in long-haul situations like these, we tend to withdraw into self-imposed isolation. We refuse to discuss the matter with our friends; we stop going to parties; if we continue attending church, we are among the first out of the building after the service.

Somehow, we figure loneliness is better than rejection. So we shy away from opening up to those who are capable of hurting us with their rejection. And there is a real possibility some of our friends will reject us. Compassionate ministry in long-term situations like these requires committed friends willing to stick with us for a long time, willing to invest heaping helpings of emotional energy, and willing to put up with us on those days we're especially difficult to live with.

Yes, our friends can reject us. But the reason we can't turn and run from them is that those same people are our healers. God uses friends to help us.

Tammy, a friend of ours, is newly divorced. My wife, Linda, bumped into her in the grocery store the other day. In gentle whispers, Tammy shared with Linda the pain of the week.

Her husband, a minister, had broken the vows of their marriage by sleeping with another woman. Tammy was heartbroken, confused, and worried about how her job as a store clerk was going to support her and her two children.

Tammy cried. And Linda cried.

There was healing in those moments. Not a cure. But healing toward the cure. And this happened not only because Linda was willing to give, but because Tammy was open to the help and encouragement that was hers for the taking.

5. *Trust your friends.* You've probably been burned before when you trusted someone. And you may get burned again. But trust, you must. You can't live without it anymore than you can live without love.

Love "always trusts, always hopes, always perseveres" (1 Corinthians 13:7). Jesus, himself, was the perfect model of one who trusted His friends. Of His disciples, He said, "I no longer call you servants . . . Instead, I have called you friends" (John 15:15). And what did Christ's friends do when he was being tried and crucified? They hid.

But to those same people, His friends, He entrusted the most important job in human history. And if His friends failed, if they let Him down, everything He had worked for, suffered for, and died for could have come to nothing. Calvary and the Resurrection could have been lost in volumes of ancient trivia.

Now that's trust.

And today, He trusts me. In spite of the many times I've let Him down, He trusts me.

Somehow, trusting my friends doesn't seem so dangerous anymore. Somehow, it just seems like the right thing to do.

14

Chapter 2

The Trauma of Moving

by C. Ellen Watts

Background Scripture: Genesis 12:1-9; Exodus 3:1-10; 4:13

IT USED TO BE THAT BIRTH and burial records for any given family could be found in a single county courthouse. Not so these days. In fact, this year, if trends continue, one North American family out of six will move.

While many long distance moves are caused by company transfers, people also relocate for career or economic reasons, job loss, or adventure. In addition, a broken home forces at least half the dissolved partnership to live elsewhere.

Traumas You Will Face

It is not uncommon for an expanding company to ignore even legitimate family needs. When a job change or divorce prompts a move, a sense of loss is inevitable. Even independently planned moves can be unspeakably painful. Because the collective and individual roots of family members are vulnerable, the escalating cost of real estate can be the least among many of the problems of moving.

The family's provider (usually Dad) is often the most likely candidate for trauma. He must learn a new job, please a different supervisor, or adjust to new territory. The change from field to office or small shop to factory, for example, can be a major adjustment. At the same time, the breadwinner must deal with home hassles, not the least of which may be a complaining spouse and children. Stress level is uncommonly high, and too few hours are available for rest or recreation. Worry over a job or an unwanted move can cause what may appear to be unrelated physical or emotional problems, including asthma, impotence, or depression.

"When you packed the rocking chair, was an elderly gentleman sitting in it?"

Depression and overeating (food can seem like a girl's best friend) are high on the list to plague women who may be less than delighted over a move. While the number of women accepting job-related transfers is on the rise, it is nearly always the wife who must seek new employment. If her position has been fulfilling, and nothing comparable is available, the resulting loss of freedom can rankle. When a spouse must report for work in advance, it is also more often the wife who must, for weeks or even months, cope with countless details. Because of either the absence or preoccupation of her mate, she must endure loneliness, make solo decisions, and cope with the fluctuating moods of the children. While childless couples or the unmarried may have less to deal with, their very aloneness can be cause for strain.

Young adults living at home must choose between two securities—the warmth of family and home, or those things that are also necessary and familiar: job, friends, and acceptance. Married children, college students, and those living alone can never return to the house where they once slept and played. An open welcome to visit, the gift of a plane ticket, or in-home entertainment privileges are some ways for parents to help meet their needs.

16

The high school years are unforgettable. Helping a nearly grown youngster cope with moving may require Solomon's wisdom, Christ's compassion, and the firmness of good old Gibraltar. Some will beg to be left behind. Grant permission to stay and finish school only if a trusted relative or friend who shares your same values is willing to take the responsibility. More often it is best to ease the pain of parting through an extra late night with friends, the promise of an occasional phone call, or simply by listening and expressing your concern.

Following a move, young people—especially teens—should be introduced quickly to group functions. Having a church to go to can help. Dealing with your teenager, the family member who is most likely to suffer adversely, may not be easy. Be aware that if good grades are not considered "in" at the new school, the adolescent may opt for D's and friends, or become a loner overnight. Listen (he may refuse to talk), and care (he may jerk away from your touch). Challenge him with a project. Some may like to decorate the new room; others will respond to possibilities for baby-sitting in the new area.

Thankfully, young children are not usually so unpredictable. But the things that upset them can be all too traumatic. Friends, pets, a yard just right for softball, all are among the trusted familiar to which a child must say good-bye. A well-adjusted child can look on a move as an exciting adventure, while at the same time he can be crushed if it means he has to miss soccer practice. A preschooler may suffer temporary upset over seeing his bed dismantled and then stop whining the moment it is out of sight. Security for young children has little to do with place and almost everything to do with familiar items and people.

Indelibly fixed in my mind is the memory of my first grandchild, chubby hands covering her face, skinny back to the wall, as she slid into a dejected heap and sobbed, "You never will come back, will you?"

We had already moved from a few blocks away to over 250 miles away. The occasion was the saying of good-byes following our first visit back. For at least 100 bleak miles of sagebrush, I could not swallow the lump in my throat; the pain of leaving loved ones affects all age levels. The examples here are typical of those moving traumas that were upsetting to my family:

• A half-grown kitten went berserk in the car, the nearest animal shelter was closed for the night, so the kitten had to be left in a cage provided for such emergencies. Although there was food and water and shade, our kindergartner prayed for at least a year that her kitty had found a good home.

• The five words penetrated through wrenching sobs: "But, Mama, I love him." She was our high school senior who later dated other boys and eventually married. But at that moment, she hurt. And I hurt with her.

• Simply by moving with her parents, a fourth grader left a junior Sunday School class twosome and joined a crowd. The strangers in the new class hid from her and found other more creative ways to be naughty. The other parents didn't seem to think it could matter. But it was my daughter's first taste of peer rejection, and her self-esteem was slow to recover.

It is also hard to leave aging parents, relinquish a Sunday School class or Scout troop, or explain to a handicapped neighbor that you can no longer drive him to therapy. And it's especially hard to leave before a replacement has volunteered for that church, school, or community involvement that has claimed so much of your time and interest.

Tips on Moving Belongings

Whether you hire professional movers (your best choice for long distance moves or those with difficult access), or you depend on the help of relatives or friends, the tips here can help your move go smoothly:

• Do heavy cleaning two to six weeks in advance of a move. At the same time, sort, give away, sell, or discard unwanted items.

• Use freezer items and do not restock. Frozen foods cannot be insured in transit.

• Moving experts require one to three days to pack a

18

household, and they never crowd the boxes or skimp on packing materials. Neither should the do-it-yourselfer.

- Be aware that newsprint can ruin unwashable items.
- Mark cartons according to rooms. List items you will need right away. Take inventory as you pack.
- Remove heavy items from drawers and pack separately.
- Delay is common. Pack more clothing than you expect to need.
- Take valuables (important papers, jewelry, heirlooms) with you in your vehicle.
- Wax appliances and furniture to help prevent scratches.
- Leave appliance warranties for the next occupant, and tag those extra keys.
- Cut paper furniture forms to scale and use graph paper to plan room arrangements. The movers will bless you.

Preparing the Family Psychologically

A move can tear a family apart if the family is short on cooperation and mutual concern. The company may select time and place, but people choose the attitude. A positive outlook is a plus, humor can work wonders, and prayer is a must. Take time with the family to invite God to take charge. Through example, teach family members to voice their fears to the One who is never too busy with packing to listen.

Christians must recognize, and share with their children, that a move may be for a higher reason than that declared by Company X. God has always directed His people to go. At times He spoke boldly; more often through a desire within a heart. He places His people strategically in order to carry out His will.

"What do you suppose the Lord is trying to do?" a friend asked after both they and we were being transferred in opposite directions.

Assurance had directed my thinking for days. "I think He's scattering Christians to where there aren't many," was my reply.

If that is true, then it is imperative to accept with grace and good cheer God's plan for redistribution. Few are like Ruth who, without regret, chose a new land, culture, and religion. Abraham had to be asked, and he knew nothing of the obstacles ahead, but he knew his God, and that was sufficient. Most will relate more to Moses, who had to argue before minding God, and charting the best route out of town. The fact is, if it's the boss making the choice, it's a heap harder to recognize and accept that God would choose to work through ungodly, or at least secular, means.

Be honest. Children need to know that parents, too, experience misgivings. They will benefit from observing an attitude of quiet acceptance toward what cannot be changed. Warn them of potential negatives and offset the latter with fun-sounding positives.

The mosquitos were like vultures the year we moved to Wyoming. So we bought repellent and said that Yellowstone Park was close enough for picnicking. Promises should be made with discretion. As it turned out, tripping off to Yellowstone was not that easy. So we visited a "real" ranch, watched beavers at work, and eventually camped for a week near Yellowstone.

Help children learn about the new locale from the encyclopedia, and from books and magazines. A postcard to the Chamber of Commerce will usually bring maps and brochures. If possible, schedule a visit before you move. Snapshots (taken by you or your real estate representative) are better than no preview.

Look for opportunities both before and after a move. In Washington State we learned about irrigation and observed the growing and processing of food. The city where we now live, Salt Lake City, has cultural advantages. But even at remote "Gasfield, U.S.A.," we saw real sheepherders, sampled genuine pit barbecue, and watched wildlife feed beside our mobile home. Treat a move as an adventure, and you and your family will grow.

Adjusting to cultural differences, including foods and customs, is also important. The West, for instance, is not simply a romantic blend of cowboys and Indians. There is the Northwest, the wild west, mountain west, desert west, cult-dominated west, and several other "wests." Each is a part of the total, and yet uniquely its own. If you can hang onto a sense of adventure, living in a different environment can be really enjoyable.

Saying Good-bye

No matter how well you plan a move, it's always hard to say good-bye to that winning soccer team, the place where a child lies buried, a beloved pastor, or family and friends. It helps to recall that the same God supplies good things in ALL places, for "My God will meet all your needs according to his glorious riches in Christ Jesus" (Philippans 4:19).

Along with depending on Bible promises to see you through the hard places, take lots of snapshots, invite friends to drop by for a last good-bye, and avoid making hasty commitments. An invitation to "come see us anytime" can mean precisely that—especially if your new location is within 50 miles of Disneyland.

Tips on Getting Settled

Once a move has taken place, no one profits from looking back or from continued grumbling. True, it's hard to be ecstatic over a promotion when the sofa doesn't match the carpet and the baby-sitter is 2,000 miles away. Even food shopping can be costly and time-consuming when stores have unfamiliar names. And if trouble starts at the new school or office, nostalgia sometimes strikes. If so, a trip back can be of benefit, though it is almost always painful. For old friends will have found new ones—time and distance will have taken their toll. Once it sinks in that no one is indispensable, healing begins, and the new home will start to look better—at least to those who choose the positive path to readjustment.

An unhappy mover once snapped at my contented murmurings, "You can say that; you have your work and your church. I have nothing."

It's too bad that her mind-set prevented her from accepting my invitation to church, for of all groups it is the most likely to offer unreserved welcome. Those who settle quickly into the business of serving the Lord in a new place are probably the most contented of all movers. The person who dares to linger after the service on that first Sunday in a new church will almost always find fellowship. And it's OK socially for you to take the initiative. An invitation from the "new kid on the block" can be highly complimentary. ("Hey, you look like someone I'd enjoy getting to know better.")

Decide quickly which church you will attend and let the main criteria for selection be based on what you can do for a church rather than what you want it to do for you. Accept input from the children, but make the final choice yourself. Not even the older teens are equipped yet to decide for a whole family. One talented family of five has been church-hopping in our area since August. It is now June, which means that approximately 4½ years of combined church loyalty and service to Christ are forever lost. And all because the seventh grader cannot find a church that pleases her.

A well-adjusted mover can serve as a catalyst for these and similar families who have not fared so well with uprooting. And they can be an encouragement to a church plagued by mobility. So don't be afraid to get involved, for the church is the most stabilizing of all community ties. And it is through the church and a personal relationship with Jesus Christ that individuals or a family can find meaning for life and strength to deal with its complexities. When spiritual needs are met, all else will fall into proper perspective—including all that can adversely happen through a move.

Chapter 3

Out of a Job . . . or About to Be

by James C. Hefley

Background Scripture: Romans 8:28, 35-39; Philippians 4:10-20

HARRY IS A BIG, ROBUST, RUDDY-FACED GUY with rippling muscles and a warm, open-faced smile. The friendly scoutmaster, Sunday School teacher type with a wife, three kids, first and second mortgages on his house, and utility bills.

I met Harry one sunny April morning in Tucson. I had been booked as a communications consultant for his church and was scheduled to visit the local TV stations that day. Harry popped into the church office and overheard me asking the secretary for directions around town.

"Let me drive you—I know this town," he offered, after introducing himself. "I have nothing else to do today."

"Sure, glad to have the company," I replied and took him to the car. "You can probably cut the time in half."

Harry headed us out into the rush-hour traffic, past where some elderly folks were pulling out of a trailer park. "Snowbirds," he noted. "They live up North, come down here to winter, then go back in the spring. Must be nice not having to worry about mortgages and kids going to college."

I ventured what I had already suspected: "You're looking for a job?"

"Have been for weeks. That's how I know the town so well. I was laid off last December from the Duval Mining Company. Reckon the company couldn't beat the foreign competition."

"Arizona is having the same problem as Michigan?"

"Not from the Japanese. Our competition is in Zaire, Peru, and a few other countries. It's cheaper to buy copper overseas

23

and have it shipped here than to buy from the mine where I got laid off."

"Understanding doesn't provide much comfort, I guess."

Harry smiled grimly. "Sure doesn't. What the economists and the politicians say won't pay my mortgage."

"First time you've been laid off?"

"Second. Several years ago I made the list. We had enough to get by, and I took it as an opportunity to do something for the Lord. Happened that our church needed a bus driver just then to take the young people to a retreat. I had the time of my life. It was also one of the best times our family ever had."

"Then the mine called you back?"

"Yeah, just as they'd promised. I figured the same thing would happen this time. Last December 14 they tacked a notice on the bulletin board at the mine saying 1,820 of us would be laid off. By the time I got home, Mary had already seen it on the TV news. 'Not to worry,' I said. 'With my seniority I'm bound to be called back.'

"Thank you, sir. I find that I do my best work after having been threatened."

"We cut back on our spending, just in case. We bought presents for the kids the day after Christmas and got some super buys. Turned out to be one of our best family Christmases ever.

"By February I was getting a little restless. Then the company announced that 1,400 would be brought back in March on a seniority basis. I knew I was high enough to be included and looked forward to getting back to the old grind. Well, they took only 600 and stopped just above my seniority. That's when I hit the streets looking for another job. Hey, there's Channel 4."

We parked near the entrance of the NBC affiliate. "Mind if I come with you?" he asked. He hung on to every word as I talked with a producer about an upcoming church feature.

"Any job possibilities?" I wondered when we were back in the car.

"I qualified as a truck driver at one place. But I couldn't pay two mortgages and buy groceries on what they offered.

"Yesterday I interviewed for driving a city transit bus. The pay is better and the security looks good. I'm to take the psychological test tomorrow. I've got my hopes up."

We made another stop. "What if you don't get the bus driving job?" I asked when we were back in the car.

"Well, I'll just know the Lord has something else. Doesn't the Bible say that God will provide for His people? What's that verse in Philippians, 'My God shall supply all your need . . .'?"

"'According to his riches in glory by Christ Jesus,'" I finished.

"I reckon the Lord's unemployment fund is unlimited."

We rode on a few blocks. "If I don't get that job with the city, I sure hope the Lord will do something soon. We may have to let our house go back in a couple of weeks and rent an apartment. That'll be tough on my family. But if we have to do it, we have to do it."

"How old are your kids, Harry?" I asked, thinking it might be better to change the subject.

"One's in grade school. Two in high school. My oldest boy is due to go to college this fall. I had hoped to have some money for his tuition. As things stand, he'll have to work full time, if he can get a job.

"This being unemployed affects everybody in your family," Harry continued. "It hurts not being able to help my boy. I'd always counted on that. A man at 44 ought to be set in his career and have a little laid by to help his kid get a better education than he had."

Harry was choking up.

"You'll have to forgive me for feeling sorry for myself. Here I am with only a high school diploma and no special skill except to drive a truck and work in a copper mine. I'll tell you something that's been going through my mind. If the Lord gets me a job, any job, so I can take care of my family, I'm going to enroll in night school and retrain for one of the coming industries. You don't think it's too late for me, do you?"

"No, Harry," I said with assurance. "You're going to make it."

"God helping me, I'm going to make it. I've got to. The folks at the church are praying for me. Any my family is sticking with me all the way."

That day I learned something about the agony of unemployment from a man of faith. I also learned something about those whose faith is weak or lacking. "Some of my buddies who were laid off with me are spending their evenings in bars," Harry said sadly. "They're drowning their troubles, spending money their families need for groceries."

Unemployment can be a terribly traumatic experience. Being out of a job can shatter your self-esteem. Especially when others around you have good jobs.

Our work tells the world what we can do. Being an employed carpenter, accountant, teacher, or machinist makes us somebody in the eyes of many people. So an unemployed father was crushed at overhearing his son and another little boy talking. "My daddy's a plumber and he's strong," the young visitor bragged. To this the jobless man's son replied, "My daddy's a nothing but he's stronger."

Dr. James Gallagher, chairman of the career consulting firm in New York City that bears his name, says unemployment hits a superambitious person hardest because he "invests so much identity in his job title . . . his first question is, 'If I'm not vice president of marketing for the XYZ Company, who am I?' His next question is, 'How am I going to survive?'" He is not talking about his physical life, Dr. Gallagher says, "but the quality of the life he's built up. His third question is: 'How do I face my family? Friends? Business colleagues?' Losing a job is a terrible blow to the ego."

Albert Bragg, a jobless 33-year-old West Virginian, told a Congressional hearing on unemployment of how he had actually put a .30-.30 rifle to his head and pulled the trigger. "I guess I moved my head," he said. "I'm sorry for doing it. I just couldn't take the pressure. I was just scared." He began crying, then apologized. "I'm sorry," he sobbed. "I was proud to be a steelworker."

Not every unemployed person goes this far. Certainly not those who are only recently out of work. But those who have been jobless for months confide to counselors and friends of unprecedented financial pressure, loss of self-esteem, and family strain. One of my longtime jobless friends told me, "Lately I've been thinking of a way to kill myself that will permit my wife to collect on my insurance." This man is a professing Christian, an active worker in his church.

Hopefully, you're not this bad off. Maybe you aren't unemployed—yet. But you know your job is shaky. You've seen that your company's sales are way down. The economic forecast for your industry is poor. There's a rumor out that headquarters in New York is going to close a sister plant in another state next week, and that your plant may be next.

If you have advance knowledge, don't wait for the ax to fall before you get started on a new plan. It's always easier to find other work while you're still working. You have a better image value to prospective employers. You have more bargaining leverage when you aren't perceived as being desperate. And you're better equipped psychologically and financially.

If you've received final notice or have just collected your last paycheck, you may not be in a healthy emotional state. Still you must make yourself do certain necessities before trying to get your act together. After you've taken care of the paperwork at your old office or plant, go to the unemployment office and file for benefits. Put in your appliciation for food stamps. If this hurts your pride, think of it as getting back a little of your tax money. But do it now, for the wheels of bureaucracy can move maddeningly slow.

Joan, a young mother of two whose company went bankrupt, told me, "We worked day and night to keep the company afloat. We let our paychecks slide for several weeks, hoping that sales might improve. When the owners finally declared bankruptcy, I needed money for groceries, like last month. My back pay wasn't a secured debt. I lost it all. I ran down to the unemployment and food stamp offices, expecting to get help immediately. I almost died when they told me how long it would be. 'How am I going to feed my kids?' I screamed at the women in the food stamp office. She shrugged and said in a tired monotone, 'Try the Salvation Army.'"

After you've done what you have to do, put in a job application at a couple of places, just for the peace of mind of knowing that your line's in the water. Then take a little time to cool off and formulate a battle plan.

Psychologists say that a suddenly unemployed person is likely to go into shock. "How can this have happened to me?" he asks. "Why must my family have to suffer from crummy management that let the company go under, outrageous union demands that priced us out of the market, stupid government cutbacks that robbed us of new contracts?" Your blood boils every time to think of what happened. You grind your teeth while trying to fix the blame.

You may feel used, betrayed, taken for a ride, discarded, especially if the company kept promising that things would get better and then suddenly announced that disaster had come. You can't sleep. You feel anxious all the time. You snap at your family over the least provocation.

Get out of the house. Go fishing. Go on retreat. Go anywhere to get away from THE PROBLEM for a few hours or days. But don't spend much time alone. Find someone you can talk to with whom you can be natural, someone who is a good listener. But not one of your old work buddies who's in the same pit you are and doesn't know how he will get out.

Remember the old spiritual, "Steal Away." Now is the time to "steal away to Jesus." He will raise your self-esteem and give you the best identification and security man can know. Then it can be said: "Now you belong to Christ Jesus, and though you once were far away from God, now you have been brought very near to him because of what Jesus Christ has done for you with his blood" (Ephesians 2:13, TLB). You will "know that all that happens to [believers] is working for our good if we love God and are fitting into his plans" (Romans 8:28, TLB).

He promises to meet the needs of His children. Needs, not wants. He never saws us off on a "limb." If He asks us to take risks, He'll follow behind to hold us. Transfer to Him your heavy burden of low self-confidence, uncertainty, and fear.

After you have prayed, do not sit and wait for the sparrows to bring you food. Take advantage of whatever means are available. God provides through all channels. He is Lord of all the earth, including friends, your church, and the social programs of the government.

He also expects you to budget, plan, and use the wisdom He will give as you have need. Sit down with your spouse and review the family finances. List your absolute necessities and fixed expenses: house payment or rent, car payment, insurance, utilities, food, minimum installment payments, medical bills, church gifts, and so forth. Add up whatever income you can count on while out of work, such as your spouse's salary, if working; unemployment insurance; severance pay; investment interest. If you have savings, postpone any withdrawals as long as you can.

If you're out of balance, trim a few dollars off the bill of each creditor and write each one, asking permission to pay the reduced amount. Most will probably go along. Then consider how you might cut back on food (powdered milk for whole milk, for example) and other items considered essential.

If your children are past infancy, let them know what the

family must do. They will probably take the cutbacks better than you think. Allow them to pray with you for a job. Keep everyone informed of what is happening.

Suppose you find you still can't make it? Perhaps the creditors won't cooperate. Perhaps the bills are just too many and too widely scattered. Visit a credit counseling agency, not a finance company where you may lose a great deal by consolidating your bills. Your pastor, United Fund agency, or any social worker can tell you where to get help. The credit counselor will divide your funds available for paying bills among your creditors and try to secure their cooperation.

In dire need, ask your pastor if your church has an emergency fund. Most churches do. You may have friends who will help, but you must let them know. When you do seek a loan from a friend or relative, offer to sign a promissory note that pledges you to pay back in specific installments or a lump sum.

A member of my Sunday School class, a major executive in a large company, recalled a time when he was down and out. "I went to see a couple of friends and told them my problem. The first one prayed with me. The second pulled out his checkbook and said, 'How much do you need?' When you're down, you find out who your friends really are."

Let's talk about looking for a job. When my friend Hal got his pink slip, he ran for a newspaper. Day after day he scanned the classifieds, making telephone calls, mailing out résumés, going for occasional interviews, doing what most job-seekers do.

Zero. Day after day he drew a blank. All the while the bills mounted. The news got around his church that Hal needed a job. A couple of hot tips and he had employment—not what he really wanted, but something to keep him going while he continued to look for better.

Check the classifieds, register at your state unemployment office, and visit employment agencies. But remember, 80 percent of all available jobs never see daylight in these places. Most of the best jobs don't even reach company personnel departments. Even then, you might be beaten out by the friend of an employee.

Hal, for example, was sure after one interview that he had a good job. Good pay and just what he wanted. When the personnel man didn't call back, Hal called him and was told, "Sorry, but when I talked to you, I didn't know that the manager in that division had already hired his wife's uncle."

Repeat 10 times for your future benefit: THE BEST JOB LEADS WILL COME FROM PEOPLE I KNOW—MY CONTACTS. Repeat a hundred times if necessary.

As self-employed writers, Marti and I are constantly asked, "How do you get your books published?" The answer is simply *contacts*. In the 19 years I've been a full-time writer, I've never placed an ad seeking work.

We believe and so pray that the Lord will lead us to the right people. We then take steps to open the door. We propose an idea for a book to an editor. If we don't know the editor, we find somebody who does and will give us an introduction.

If you're out of work, time is not a surplus commodity. You've got to make the right connection soon. So start making your list of people who might be job leads. Your brother-in-law might have an old college roommate who is manager at a place you'd like to work. Get the guy's name. Ask him if he has anything open. If he doesn't, ask if he has any suggestions.

After asking relatives, next check with close friends and neighbors. Look at your Christmas card list. Review old school yearbooks. Jot down the names of old school buddies. That red-headed jokester you used to double-date with might be just the person to put you on a rocket for the future.

While you're job-looking, read up on how to prepare résumés and succeed in interviews. Here are some pointers from the experts for a professional résumé:

1. *Keep it simple, short, and well organized.* No longer than two pages.

2. *Be honest without putting yourself down.* Be prepared if you're asked to document what you've written down.

3. *Tailor the résumé to the job.* Identify and underline skills you think will help you on this job or with this company.

4. *List achievements and awards that are pertinent.* The company probably doesn't care to know that you won a $25.00

savings bond for answering a trivia question from a radio station. The company *will* be interested to know that you qualified for the college scholastic society in your field.

5. *Mention volunteer experience if skills relate to the job.*

6. *Leave off these items:* No photos unless specifically required. No personal information unless directly relevant to the job. This includes age, height, weight, marital status, religious affiliations, and so forth. Omit negative reasons for leaving an earlier job. Don't give references unless you can list a person well known in the field in which you are applying. Just say, "References provided upon request."

7. *Include a personal letter of application.* Simply and briefly request consideration for the position, mention reasons you are interested, and ask for a personal interview.

The résumé is a screening mechanism for the employer and a door opener for you. After a few days, follow it up with a phone call or a short note stating that you really would like an interview.

Now for some tips on the interview:

1. *Do your homework.* Research the company, its products, services, and place in the industry.

2. *Prepare for standard questions.* The inteviewer says, "Tell me about yourself," and you begin, "I was born . . . I went to school at . . ." How much better is: "I've become very interested in . . . I've discovered I have some real ability in . . . I have some special training in . . ."

Another stock question is, "Why did you leave your last job?" Negative comments will only weigh in against you. If the company closed because of foreign competition, say so. And you might add. "From that experience I got some ideas that I believe will help this company."

Make a list of questions you expect. Have your spouse or a friend interrogate you. But don't go in with a memorized spiel. Just be ready to express yourself in a positive way that will indicate your knowledge of the company and awareness of abilities in yourself that will advance the firm. Remember, the interviewer is not running an aid office. He's trying to help his company. If he thinks you can make a solid contribution, then you could get the job.

3. *Be assured.* Get a good night's sleep the night before the interview. Eat a hearty breakfast. Read over your résumé and information about the company. Arrive ahead of time so you will have time to relax and review your ideas over a cup of coffee. It's like taking a final exam in college. If you're confident you will pass, you probably will.

4. *Dress properly.* A traditional business suit and white shirt are almost always in style for a man seeking a white-collar position. For a blue-collar job, you could not go wrong by wearing a tie. A conservative but fashionable suit or skirt and blouse would be safe for a woman. Generally try to avoid distracting clothing, hairstyles, and jewelry. You want the interviewer to hear and see you, not what you're wearing.

5. *Act normal and establish rapport.* If the interviewer wants to talk football for a couple of minutes, go along. But try to stay on safe subjects for small talk. You're taking chances by volunteering your opinion on politics and controversial social issues. Be personable without trying to become instant buddies. Use last names and proper *titles*. If the interviewer is a "doctor," address him as such.

6. *Be straightforward, honest, and pleasant.* Look the interviewer in the eye. Answer questions forthrightly.

7. *Keep the emphasis on what you can do for the company, not what the company can do for you.* Don't ask about salary, vacations, or pensions in the initial interview. If the interviewer asks you to specify your salary needs, say or write "Negotiable." Avoid boxing yourself in.

8. *Act enthusiastic but not anxious.* If you've researched the prospective employer, you can show intelligent enthusiasm. It doesn't hurt to brag (honestly) on the company. Just don't give the impression that getting the job is a life-or-death matter for you. You want the interviewer to feel that if the company doesn't get you, it will be the loser.

9. *Send a thank-you letter after you get home.* Briefly re-emphasize your interest and enthusiasm for the job. Thank the interviewer for his time. Offer to answer any further questions.

10. *Follow up in a week if you haven't heard.* A short note may be better than a phone call, which might give the impression that you're pestering the interviewer. Simply say you're wondering how things are going. Wish the interviewer well. Don't make any demands.

If your first interview doesn't pan out, use the expertise you've gained to do better the next time. Don't take each no as a personal defeat. Keep your chin up. Keep writing letters, sending out résumés, and making phone calls.

Above all, maintain closeness with the Lord. Allow Him to walk with you. Scripture says: "Whether therefore ye eat, or drink, or whatsoever ye do, do all to the glory of God" (1 Corinthians 10:31, KJV). The job you want, the income you need is for the glory of the Lord. If you really want to please Him, He will sustain you until you find the job He has for you.

From *Life Changes* by James Hefley. Published by Tyndale House Publishers, Inc., © 1984 by James Hefley. Used by permission.

Chapter 4

Working Through Loneliness

by Larry Jones

Background Scripture: Genesis 2:18-25; Hebrews 13:5b

FOUR O'CLOCK CAME, but no Mrs. Wortham.

I had been anticipating her arrival since 3:45, so each minute past the time she was expected seemed even longer. At 4:15, I left the office and walked past the receptionist's desk, hoping to find her. Failing to see her I strode back through the building to the parking lot in the rear.

Amy was sitting in her car. She saw me but made no effort to get out. Without comment, I opened the door and got in beside her. Finally she broke the silence, both hands on the wheel, looking ahead as though she were driving.

"Rev. Jones, I am a very, *very* lonely woman. You might say I am a lonely old woman, but it isn't the age that distinguishes me—only the loneliness. My children are gone, my mother is gone, and my husband is rarely at home. But that isn't it.

"I'm lonely when I'm eating out with other women. That feeling never leaves. When I go to a party, it's there. When I shop in a crowded store, loneliness goes with me. Wherever I go, there is this void that swallows me up. It almost speaks to me . . . reaches out to me. I can almost see it. I can't touch it but, oh, can I feel it!

"When I'm alone, as I have been this past hour, I am so keenly aware of it. I even say out loud, 'I am lonely.'"

I started to address her as "Mrs. Wortham," but caught myself, thinking how impersonal it sounded.

"At the risk of sounding trite, you must know you are not alone in your sense of loneliness," I began slowly and quietly.

"Loneliness afflicts both men and women, those of status as well as the derelicts, the adolescents and the aged, the single and the married, the learned and the illiterate—and I might add, even the clergy—not to mention those forgotten by society in prisons or hospitals or on skid row. No, you are not alone in your loneliness."

I was fishing. I did not want to lecture, just to listen—to talk *with* her, not *to* her. But failing to get a foothold, I forged

ahead, hoping to find some conversational pivot that might cause her to say, "I hadn't thought of it that way."

"The frightening part is that our society is set up to exploit the lonely—to create situations to attract the lonely. We have dance studios, health salons, and private parties for the purpose of meeting people. Our society is filled with those who traffic in boredom—those who profit from promising that time will be consumed for those who pay the price.

"On every corner there's a bar, where night after night the same people sit side by side on rows of stools—monuments to loneliness."

Amy continued to stare straight ahead as I continued. "Even prostitution and homosexuality become escapes from loneliness for all involved—both the one buying and the one selling. All these endeavors become dead ends, though, because they fill time, but not the void."

She relaxed her hands from the grip of the wheel. Leaning her head back against the seat, eyes closed, she looked like a little girl.

"How does one fill the void?" Amy's voice came barely above a whisper. It seemed she wanted to say more, but didn't because the effort would be too great. She appeared tired rather than engulfed with emotion. In fact, the lack of emotion was almost chilling.

Maybe I was reading too much into the setting. It occurred to me that this could be her way to solve loneliness—to spend time seeking out a listening ear. Perhaps I was taking everything too serious, looking for the dramatic. After all, I knew little about her . . . nothing except what she had told me.

"Perhaps another drink would help," I baited. She had hinted in our phone conversation that she had been drinking. So I brought it up—still fishing for an approach to take with our discussion.

"Don't think I didn't consider it," she mumbled, eyes still closed.

"Maybe a drink would help you to forget that your loneliness is not the absence of others, but your presence among others where it is treated as absence," I said bluntly.

"Perhaps another drink will help you forget that you are regarded as dead. Perhaps another drink will let you forget you are forgotten."

I was looking for a fight—an argument—anything that would put life in her.

"I'm not an alcoholic, Rev. Jones, at least not yet. But I could be very easily. In fact, I might welcome it."

Her words faded into a wry, humorless laugh. "Forgotten, eh? Regarded as dead? I should be so lucky! The truth is, I don't consider myself *regarded* at all. Only the void is real. So what else can you suggest besides a drink, *Rev. Jones?*"

She used my name with the same careful intent that I had avoided hers. There was at least a little fight left in her.

"You might consider sex. At least you will not be alone, though you probably will still be lonely," I shot back.

She smiled, her eyes still closed. Amy was still a beautiful woman, and she knew it.

"Is that a proposition, preacher?"

I let the question pass. She knew it wasn't offered seriously and needed no response.

"You've tried marriage. Is this a part of your problem or your solution? You have told me nothing of your husband."

"My marriage is not worth the paper it's written on. What is there to tell? He's a successful man; self-made, self-motivated, self-centered; spends half his time away working and the other half just away. What happens to me is neither because of him nor despite him. I don't love him—I don't hate him. How we drifted apart is not the incredible thing, but how we ever got together. How can two teenagers make promises to each other with any assurance that they can or will want to keep them 25 years later?"

This wasn't the time or place for marital counseling. No use trying to make two into one if you cannot make one into one.

"You can always seek out counseling. Maybe if we search your past long enough, we can find someone you can blame yourself on."

She opened her eyes and glared at me. "I'm beginning to think I made a poor choice, Rev. Jones. So far you've only made snide suggestions, which we both know have nothing to do with what we're talking about. Surely you can do more than prey on what little you know about me!"

A spark.

"And then, of course, you can always pity yourself. Why not? Everybody else does."

She settled back, her hands on the wheel.

"I suppose self-pity does figure in. But what else is there ... when no one else ..."

She turned, facing me.

"Rev. Jones, do you have a first name? Larry. Larry Jones. Right? Larry, can you give me 10 practical things a person might do to overcome loneliness? Let's just suppose you were assigning homework for a child," she snapped.

"Certainly I could if I thought it would do any good."

She reached in her purse and took a dollar bill in her hand. "I'll give you a dime for each one."

I had misgivings about the exercise, but I felt she was buying time—time that I needed as much as she.

"First, make plans to see three people you have known and liked but have lost contact with," I began. "Second, make a list of your interests in an effort to uncover a hobby. Third, make a list of people you know who are lonely and ask each of them to do something with you. Fourth, write letters to three old friends you have neglected. Fifth, do one good turn for someone each day. Sixth, be on the lookout for new places to go. Seventh, always have something to look forward to. Eighth, don't expect too much too soon. Ninth, deal with your loneliness a bit at a time. Find ways to get through an hour ... and then a day."

"And 10?"

"Nine is all I know, and I don't have change so you can keep your dollar."

She was leaning back again, eyes closed.

"Larry Jones, you can't offer things like those to a basket

39

case. Surely there's more in that head of yours than trying to turn a middle-aged misfit into a pen pal."

"There's more, Amy, if you are willing to accept your solitude and build on it."

"Such as?"

"Such as this for starters: You are alone and yet you are never alone."

She was looking at me again, and it was I who leaned back with eyes closed.

"Let me tell you about a friend of mine," I continued. "The rumor was that He was born out of wedlock . . . which wasn't true, but He had to grow up with it nonetheless. He was completely misunderstood by His parents. He became a minister but was later disowned by His church. In time, His friends left Him. One of His best friends betrayed Him.

"He was later falsely accused on criminal charges, tried and sentenced to death. During His excution, He even thought He was forsaken by God. He died with His mother weeping at His side.

"He spent most of His adult life alone, forsaken by friends, family, and peers. And all He ever accomplished was to alter the history of the human race. For he built His life on a promise . . . that He would never leave Amy Wortham alone. Never. Never forsake her. Always stay beside her . . . guide her . . . comfort her."

She laid her head in her hands on the steering wheel.

"Oh, Larry . . ." She began to cry. "If only . . ." The tears came faster.

"Amy, Jesus loves you. He cares for you. I know this doesn't fill up all the empty space this very moment. But He can fill the void in your life if you will only let Him."

She stopped crying and reached in her purse for her handkerchief.

"I must go, I really must."

"But, Amy . . ."

"Please."

I opened the door. "It's been a long day. Amy, I feel I have known you a long time. And do you realize it's still only Monday? Will you come back in the morning? Nine o'clock?"

"Yes, I'll be here. But I must go now."

I got out of the car, shut the door, and started walking away.

"Larry."

"Yes?" Turning toward her.

"Thanks."

Chapter 5

A Parent's Shattered Dreams

by Guy Greenfield

Background Scripture: Psalm 42:1-11; Romans 5:1-5

OUR CULTURE TEACHES us to dream, to plan for our children's future. Although our dreams may be somewhat unrealistic, they are important to us and contain a degree of pleasure in the dreaming process itself. However, dreams can be shattered on the reefs of reality. Things don't always turn out as we had hoped. Yet we are seldom prepared for this.

Those Early Years

Phil and Constance Fisher were extremely pleased and proud when Jeff was born. Their dreams for him included every possible ambition. They took seriously the vows they made in church the Sunday Jeff was dedicated to the Lord on parent-and-child dedication day. Surely, they dreamed, he would grow up to become an outstanding Christian person in whatever vocation he might choose for himself. They dreamed he would one day marry a Christian woman and discover the joys of his own Christian family.

These were big dreams, covering many years. Maybe it would have been enough at first just to dream of the happy days that Jeff would experience as an infant, boy, and young man before he left home. However, broad or long-range the dreams, it is normal for parents like the Fishers to aspire to noble goals for their children.

Parents always desire that their children be healthy in both body and mind and that they stay that way as they grow up. Christian parents certainly dream of the day when each child accepts Jesus Christ as his Savior and continues growing in the knowledge of God and the Christian way of life.

The Years of Fulfillment

In time the Fishers saw many of their dreams for Jeff come true. In his preschool years he was a pleasant child who generally responded well to Phil and Constance. He received what most parents would have considered an adequate amount of

love and attention. Morever, it seemed that he responded well to the discipline of his parents.

Jeff's grade school years seemed fairly typical. There were a few problems at school, but nothing particularly serious or long-standing. He seemed to get along well with the other children, and his schoolwork was above average. At age 10, Jeff made a profession of faith in his church, was baptized, and continued in all the activities that the church offered for children his age. He would pray at home along with all the other members of the family. He knew what it meant to own and regularly read his Bible.

By the time Jeff reached junior high school, he was well on his way to fulfilling his parents' dreams for him. The Fishers' expectations of Jeff were being fairly well fulfilled even by the time he reached high school. There were a few disciplinary bumps along the way but nothing serious.

Early Signs of Rebellion

Years later the Fishers could look back on Jeff's development and see some early signs of rebellion. They could remember catching him lying about something, but this didn't happen very often. They could recall times when he would take something that didn't belong to him. This too was not a regular thing.

The thing that bothered the Fishers the most was Jeff's growing independence. He had a mind of his own and could think for himself. This especially worried Phil when Jeff would not do exactly what he was told to do. Phil's reaction to Jeff's "insubordination" (Phil had been in the Marines) was often harsh and extreme. Phil used his belt quite often, especially during Jeff's junior high school years.

It seems that the Fishers failed to understand the natural process of a child growing up and cutting the cords with his parents. Although the cutting should be a gradual process, it does need to take place. It usually begins in the preteen years and accelerates through adolescence.

There are two possible misdirections a child can go in this process of cutting the cords. One is for the cords to be cut too soon, either by irresponsible parents or by a stubborn, rebellious child. This process would be much like a student pilot being sent up on his first solo flight so soon that he would likely end his flying career earlier than expected.

The second possible misdirection is for parents to resist cutting the cords for as long as possible. This may produce either a rebellious child (both nature and culture tell him to cut the cord as soon as self-confidence allows) or an excessively dependent, anxious, and fearful child who has no self-confidence. The uncut-cord people are as much a problem to society as the rebellious ones.

The so-called early signs of rebellion may actually be expressions of the natural process of growing up: achieving independence and self-confidence. The Fishers later admitted that they failed to recognize this in Jeff and overreacted with harshness and anger. They felt they would lose control otherwise.

The Invasion by the Peer Group

The peer group usually emerges during the junior high school years, although it may appear earlier. This group of friends of about the same age, certainly from the same grade in school, comes into a person's life in an innocent process. It is normal for a boy or girl to want friends. During the preteen and teen years the desire to belong becomes quite strong.

The function of the peer group is to assist the youth to cut the cords of the family and achieve independence. The peer group actually becomes a temporary second family, in competition with the family into which a person is born.

The major problem with the peer group comes when it represents values and a life-style sharply opposed to and in conflict with those of one's family. Susan Wallace chose a peer group in high school that expressed moral values strongly in opposition to those of her family. Her peer group approved of illicit sexual relations, drinking alcoholic beverages, profanity, and a disrespectful attitude toward religion.

Jeff Fisher also identified with a secular, pleasure-oriented peer group during his junior high school years. In time this group of boys began experimenting with drugs. In order for Jeff to be accepted, he had to conform to the group's behavior. One thing led to another as the pressure to belong mounted. Before long, Jeff was smoking pot and popping pills. If "everybody [the peer group] is doing it" and you're not, then what's wrong with you? To be accepted, you have to conform. In his efforts to achieve independence, Jeff discovered that he had become the unwitting victim of a new dependence, the peer group.

Unfortunately, neither Susan's nor Jeff's churches provided vital, attractive Christian peer groups. The secular, anti-Christian peer groups of the public school system had invaded the families of the Wallaces and the Fishers and had won.

Other Counterinfluences

It would be a mistake to conclude that the peer group was the only threat to Susan's and Jeff's Christian upbringing. Other counterinfluences had been at work, slowly, subtly, yet effectively.

Television is certainly a major force in the lives of today's youth. It has been estimated that by the time one reaches the age of 18 today, he has been exposed to more than 15,000 hours of television viewing since birth. This is quite a contrast to the experience of this author who, although born in 1931, did not see a television set until he was 18 and did not own one until he was 25.

The effect of television on today's youth has without doubt been tremendous. Although television is not all bad, from a Christian perspective, it has obviously presented alternative life-styles and values for youth to consider. Much of its secular influence has been subtle. Illicit sex, the use of alcohol, and even violence often have been presented with an attitude of approval. If parents quietly condone such presentations, youth may conclude that such practices are acceptable for them also.

Magazines, books, and movies, along with the lyrics of youth-oriented music, certainly can convey messages that counter the Christian way of life. Many youth have accepted these secular messages as their own.

Another influence that has adversely affected some youth who have regularly attended church is certain disappointments

46

in the life of the church. During her high school years, Susan Wallace's church had a youth director who became sexually involved with one of the church's teenagers. The exposure of his behavior played a major role in Susan's graded disenchantment with the church. This sort of thing happens more often than church leaders prefer to admit. Although most youth survive such shocking news, some do not. It can be the final "push out the door" toward another value system.

When the Dreams Begin to Disintegrate

When Constance Fisher was cleaning out 15-year-old Jeff's chest of drawers one day and found a marijuana cigarette, her early dreams for Jeff began to disintegrate. Was this just a teenage fling on Jeff's part? Was it merely the result of natural curiosity? Or did it signal something seriously wrong?

Soon after Susan began dating Chuck, Betsy Wallace had found a container of contraceptive foam in Susan's room. In answer to her mother's questions, Susan pleaded ignorance about how the container got there. She speculated that one of her girl friends left it in the room as a joke. With Betsy, as with Constance, disturbing questions flooded her mind. Is Susan telling the truth? If not, how far has she really gone with Chuck? Or is this just the result of a high school senior's curiosity about such things? Could it be the signal of something more than just curiosity?

There's a Lot You Don't Know

Living with growing, active, curious, intelligent, and inquisitive teenagers often presents a major problem of trust versus distrust between parent and youth. Parents want to be able to trust their children. Distrust is a painful experience. Yet many youth know that in their experimentation with life, in their testing of the moral limits of their family's values, if they tell their mothers or fathers everything they think or do, then they will be punished or restricted in their behavior.

Rather than face such consequences, youth often choose to hide the facts and keep their secrets. Besides, parents cannot monitor all the thoughts and actions of their children. The best that parents can do is to be consistent in their own behavior, as well as to trust their children to live up to the best they were taught. Even then there's a lot you don't know about your children's behavior. Your only resource is to place your children in God's hands—God, who loves them so much more than human parents could ever love.

The Shattering and Its Trauma

When Constance and Phil received a phone call from the police that 16-year-old Jeff had been arrested for possession of illegal drugs and was being detained at the police department, their dreams were thoroughly shattered. It was not the end of the world for the Fishers, but their dreams were broken on the hard rocks of reality.

When Betsy and Arthur learned of Susan's pregnancy, their dreams also were shattered. In their long-laid plans to rear a wonderful Christian girl, in their efforts to guide such plans to fulfillment, something had gone wrong. It seemed that the whole endeavor of 18 years had failed.

The trauma experienced by the Fishers and the Wallaces cannot be described in words. Only those couples who go through this know what it's like. The best that can be said by way of description is this: it hurts, it's hard, and it's debilitating. There is no feeling quite like the feeling of parental failure.

Dare We Dream Again?

Both the Wallaces and the Fishers expected their children to grow up and be like them. Their earliest dreams were dreams patterned after their own experiences and ambitions. Their children didn't turn out that way. The dreams were broken. Therefore, they wondered, dare we dream again?

It is natural for parents to want the best for their children, but the fact remains that our children are going to turn out to be what they want to be and not what we want them to be. These may be very different goals. But children have the right to decide for themselves what they will become.

This is hard for many parents to accept. They often feel

that they have the age and experience to determine the direction their children should go. Yet people like the Wallaces and Fishers are learning that their personal examples of daily living are the best they can offer their children.

If the moral values and religious beliefs of parents are in any sense superior, better, or more meaningful than those of other people, then the children will have to discover this for themselves. This may mean discovery by way of experimental comparison of alternative life-styles, painful as that sometimes is.

Getting Worse Before Getting Better

As you read this, you may be in the midst of a traumatic experience with your own son or daughter. You want and are seeking help. I hope this chapter helps you. But I want to warn you now: things may get worse before they get better.

You are going to need a lot of patience. You may need to radically change your usual approaches to your child. He may not be through testing the new and different life-styles. Sometimes the testing has to run its course, much like a virus.

There may be days when you feel you can take it no more: a day when your son is sentenced by a court, a day when your daughter is suspended from school in April of her senior year of high school, a day when you haven't heard from your runaway daughter in more than four months and don't know whether she is dead or alive, a day when your 16-year-old son is visited by your church's youth minister and your son tells the minister to "go to hell" for no apparent reason other than that he doesn't want to attend church anymore.

Yes, your situation may get worse before it gets better. But, believe me, it can get better.

From *The Wounded Parent*, by Guy Greenfield. Published by Baker Book House, © 1982 by Guy Greenfield. Used by permission.

Chapter 6

When the Marriage Begins to Wither

by Jan Frye

Background Scripture: Colossians 3:12-19

I WANTED TO TELL HAL. But his meeting would begin in 20 minutes, so he had to run.

"We'll talk when I get home," he said.

By eleven o'clock I couldn't stay awake another minute. I hardly even remembered our good-night kiss.

The next morning I showered while he jogged three miles. Then we met in the kitchen for breakfast.

Peering into my glass of milk, I began, "I need to tell you something, Honey."

"Oh, yeah . . . what is it?" He chomped into buttered wheat toast.

"I miss you," I said, still staring at my milk.

Hal leaned back and laughed. "We see each other every day!"

"I still miss you," I said quietly.

"What do you mean, you miss me?"

I couldn't find the words. How could I explain to to Hal that I sensed our relationship was ever so slowly . . . dying? I stammered with, "Well, we don't see each other as much . . . as much as married people should. And when we are together, well, we just talk about what's going on."

"What else is there to talk about?" he asked.

My voice cracked. "How about talking about our love?"

"I love you. You love me. We know that. We say it every day."

No, no, no. I didn't want another fruitless conversation

that dead-ended with both of us thinking surely there's nothing wrong because we're Christians.

Twenty-one years later, still married, I understand better why couples—some Christian and some non-Christian—either grow apart or grow closer.

If love is an unselfish, giving expression of deep appreciation for another person, as Dr. James Dobson says, then I suppose I can commit myself toward keeping love alive. But how?

I recalled a Christian couple who recently faced Hal and me in a marriage accountability session. The husband began with, "First, we admit that our marriage is in trouble." I admired his openness as he stated the bitter truth. Facing the truth, even the truth that their marriage needed work, began to set this couple free.

Hurting marriages can resemble anything from a head cold to brain cancer. Some need minor healing; others, major healing. Only after a couple honestly sees their need for a repair, can healing begin. Love can grow.

Not long ago I listened while Gary and Jean, a Christian couple married for 15 years, stepped toward healing.

"I—I want you to forgive me," she said, "for arguing with

"Howard?"

you about how to discipline the kids. Maybe we can talk and come up with some new ideas together. But I don't want to hurt you anymore by arguing."

Without hesitation, Gary forgave and embraced her, asking her forgiveness, too. Even the "head cold" sort of marriage trouble needs to be honestly recognized and forgiven before love can flourish.

While growing up, some of us began observing and imitating others who taught us, often unknowingly, how to communicate clearly. Some of us learned how to handle conflict constructively and how to convince others of our genuine love. Some of us learned the importance of praying together, too. But few of us learned all this well. And none of us learned these things perfectly.

"I brought so many habits, some good, some not so good, into my marriage," admitted 30-year-old Tom, "thinking my love for Shirley should melt away any conflict. Then Shirley's parents insisted that we visit them at least twice a week. But I wanted us to be more independent."

Shirley added, "Since I was afraid to keep bringing up the problem, I just stopped talking about how I resented Tom for not wanting to visit my parents. The tension built up inside me like a growing tumor."

Shirley and Tom finally recognized the truth when they openly talked together and forgave each other for their resentment. They agreed to compromise with a once-a-week quality visit as a couple. Then Shirley found other times to visit her parents during Tom's working hours. Their efforts toward better communication quite naturally resulted in a growing love for each other and for Shirley's parents.

Recently a friend shared with me that she couldn't understand why she felt unloved by her husband. She knew in her mind that George loved her very much, but he couldn't seem to communicate it in ways she needed. Betty didn't know how to talk with George about this "gray area" in their marriage, especially since he was basically a good husband. One day, though, she gathered her courage and brought up the subject.

"But I say 'I love you' several times a day," said George. "Don't you believe me?"

"I don't understand this either," said Betty. "I just know I'm drifting from you emotionally, and I can't seem to do the right things to help. Something needs to change, George, because I'm scared."

As George listened to Betty and saw how much she hurt, he decided to search for more convincing ways to express love to his wife. When they talked further, Betty still couldn't seem to pinpoint the missing ingredients. George, however, pursued in rare style for an answer. He discovered by "love expression experiments," as he called them, that Betty felt genuinely loved when he stopped reading the paper and looked at her as she spoke to him. Also, the gestures of love more commonly associated with dating—an unexpected bouquet of flowers, a walk in the moonlight, opening her car door—all worked to revive Betty's longings to feel loved again. George's "experiments" required time and effort, both of which automatically conveyed love to his wife. But his discoveries greatly enhanced their love for each other. The last time I saw them they spoke of planning a "taco date" after church. They seemed to be best friends again.

The best friends of all, I've learned, value time for just talking together. They talk not only about what they do but also of how they feel and what they're thinking, wanting, and sensing. Best friends can feel free to toss ideas back and forth, knowing that they'll be heard, and not judged or repeated to others.

"My wife and I are best friends," Hal once told a group, "and I think it's because we're free to say anything to each other. We're constantly working to encourage each other, too."

That's true. But at times Hal and I find that our least encouraging moments occur when we're tired or under time pressure. A fatigued body or mind usually reacts from a more negative perspective, we've found.

Last week our three teenagers continuously needed to be in different places at odd times. The same week, we entertained house guests, he worked overtime everyday, and I took exams at school. At night we flopped into bed, barely speaking, much less encouraging one another. I remember patting his hand and saying, "I miss you," while he groaned, "Nobody should be this busy." We knew that this was not a good week for discussing anything deeper than, "I'll see you at church." But we also knew the schedule was only temporary. Constant, more permanent fatigue and time pressure, however, places couples in a danger zone for communicating as best friends.

Writer Leslie Parrott says marriage is a loving, lifetime friendship with the added dimension of sex. Of all couples in the world, Christian couples should enjoy each other the most, and that includes the sexual relationship. Christian couples need to cultivate frankness in their private talks about what they enjoy sexually. Sometimes we mistakenly assume that our spouse can read our mind. But since our spouse cannot instinctively know everything about us sexually, we need to express what we like best. Perhaps George's idea of "love expression experiments" could spark a couple to better sexual pleasure. Or maybe a trusted professional counselor could help.

Charlie W. Shedd reports that after counseling over 2,000 couples with various needs, not one couple came to him if they regularly prayed together. Some of them "used to," he said.

Hal and I testify that our marriage turned a significant corner the day we resolved to resume daily prayers together about our specific praises and needs. Praying specifically stimulates, first of all, an honest look at our needs . . . a search for the truth in our relationship. Before praying together, we occasionally need to forgive one another. Then, through the thanksgiving and the needs we unload before Jesus, He teaches us, without fail, that He is our Strength when we fall short.

I once knew some newlyweds who struggled financially. She came from a relatively wealthy family and felt comfortable in spending money freely. His background taught him early in life to work hard and spend carefully. Needless to say, within their first few months together, they talked many times about her purchases. When the bills continued to arrive in their mailbox, although less frequently, the tension in their young marriage raised high. Then one day, with suitcase in hand, just before she headed back to her parents, they stopped and talked about their commitment, for better or for worse.

"*Worse,* to me, meant near poverty," she said later.

"To me," he said, "*worse* meant losing my wife!"

They talked about their marriage vows and made fresh commitments to cooperate and work hard together, even if it meant years of lifetime until they could afford extras. In time, they found new ways to economize. Then they committed themselves to a significant *better* regarding their finances. Since they were both tithing Christians, they decided to pray together often regarding wisdom for handling the other 90 percent.

"Praying together about money helped our attitudes so much," they said, "that we decided to start praying together about our other needs, too."

Eventually they also chose to precede prayer by reading the Bible together every night. They talk about what the scripture means to them personally and as a couple. Then they share with each other about their spiritual lives that day. Whenever I see them, I admire their discipline because I sense that their love for each other is maturing.

I can kneel with Hal and pray, "Lord, I miss Hal this week. Give him strength and wisdom as he works long hours. Thank You for his health and energy." And Hal can pray, "Give her extra grace during this tough week. Keep her patient and strong. And please remind her of my love."

When we pray together our spirits form a triangle, simultaneously moving toward each other and toward God. He truly blesses our honesty and efforts. But he is our number one Resource for keeping love alive in marriage.

Chapter 7

When You Lose Your Health
by Kenneth E. Schemmer

Background Scripture: John 9:1-7; 2 Corinthians 5:17-20; 12:7-10

IN 1959 I started my medical training because I felt God calling me to serve Him as a physician. At that time time I perceived the practice of medicine as the ultimate way to share in God's healing ministry. During succeeding years of training, I gained knowledge and skills to "help God" wherever he wanted me to.

Before my training was completed, I encountered hundreds of patients. I saw how much many of them suffered and how often they carried the burdens of their tragic situations on their own shoulders. I wondered how their diseases affected their total personalities.

I began to ask: What is the meaning of suffering? Is it even worth being human if humans have to go through such tragedies? My personal experience soon provided grist for the mill of my soul.

One early January morning, abdominal pain, vomiting, and diarrhea suddenly struck me. At first I assumed that those symptoms indicted only a minor abdominal illness. Although the vomiting and diarrhea subsided in nine hours, the pain continued. As a doctor, I wondered why I was sick. The next day my skin and eyes turned yellow. I had a diseased gall bladder and a gallstone in my bile duct.

As a Christian, I felt troubled in spirit. The pain and weakness confused and stunned me spiritually. I felt as if death were hovering over me. How can I handle this suffering if it gets any worse or doesn't let up soon? I questioned. My prayers became more serious as I talked with God about my sickness: "Lord, I don't like to feel this horrible, and I want to get well. But there must be some reason for suffering. I want to draw closer to You if I can."

As a Christian I wanted not to deny my agony but to face my problem squarely. I believed God's promise, "I will never fail you nor forsake you" (Hebrews 13:5, RSV). I asked God to give me the courage I needed to accept my suffering. I asked for the

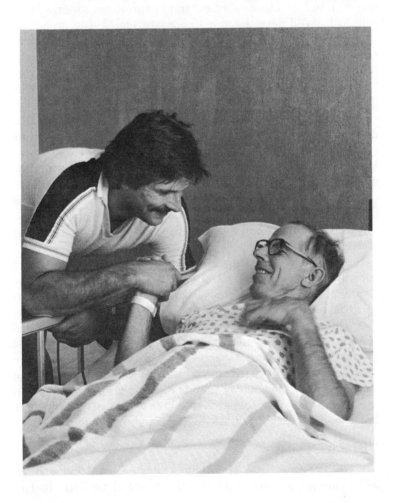

peace and joy in my soul that others needed to see in me in order to know He was still with me.

Then the tiredness started. Fatigue overcame me. Walking to and from the bathroom wore me out so much that I would sleep for hours. While the disease progressed, I questioned my motives. Which concerned me more: My health and my work as a surgeon or my relationship with Christ? I had asked that question before, but now I needed to express my love for Him, even if I would never be able to operate again.

Would God miraculously heal me, or did He want to work through His natural laws of healing and through physicians? I felt peace flooding my soul. Either I would be delivered from this suffering quickly, or He would use my suffering to help me grow as a person.

When my five-hour operation ended, I experienced the most severe physical pain of my life. I couldn't believe anything could hurt so much. I cried out, "God, where on earth are You? Why does there have to be such pain and suffering in this world?" Then I recalled that Jesus had asked the same question on the Cross, yet He had suffered and died so that the love of God might be shared with humankind. Despite my shattered physical condition and stunned psyche, by faith I rose a bit above my misery.

Nevertheless, my stuggle for complete faith in Jesus Christ continued. I recalled my weaknesses when I had problems, and I remembered my sins. I grew discouraged as I fought this great spiritual battle. Was I going to give up on God, or would I stake everything in faith on Jesus Christ? Would He keep what I had committed to Him, even through this suffering? Finally, I chose to trust myself to Christ Jesus—body, mind, and soul.

During the first five days after my operation, pain and weakness wore me out. My roommate was dying with cancer of the lung. Most of those nights he coughed excessively, trying to breathe. Each time I fell asleep, his coughing woke me.

Ultimate Trust

Despite my physical fatigue and emotional exhaustion, Jesus gave me a peace and joy that convinced me I still had an authentic spiritual life. He had sustained my commitment to Him after all. Now I knew I could trust Him even in death.

Eventually I began to recover. Each day as I gained new strength, my faith in Jesus Christ increased. I yearned to spend my time and my life for Him.

"Lord Jesus," I prayed, "I accept my situation in health or sickness and depend on You to give me wholeness. From now on I dedicate my energies to serving You. In sickness I trust You with my weaknesses and ask for energy to handle my illness. Show Your presence in my life that I might share You, whether I'm healed physically or not."

As others worked or visited with me, His spirit enlivened our relationships with fruit: love and joy, peace and forgiveness, kindness and gentleness, patience, faithfulness, and self-control.

One month after the operation I returned to my surgical training program. I had new sensitivity to the needs of my patients. Now I could anticipate many of their physical, emotional, and spiritual needs. I met those needs best when I listened to their struggles and told them about mine. I discovered the importance of treating the whole patient, not just the body. As I talked with my patients, people began to tell me what value they were finding in their suffering.

At first my sickness had appeared to be an impediment to my growth as a surgeon. When I found out I would lose at least two months' experience as chief resident, I had despaired. But the Lord knew I needed those months to gain new insights. Had God miraculously healed me, I would have lost only two weeks. A supernatural healing would have increased my faith in Him. That kind of increase in faith, however, could not be compared to the confidence in Him I had gained by going through such agony myself.

Not only can I now trust Him even in the face of death, but also I have found that true healing extends beyond the body to the patient's personhood. I can share in Christ's healing ministry by sharing His Spirit with my patients.

This sharing of Christ in our relationships was described by the apostle Paul in 2 Corinthians 5:18-20:

All this is from God, who through Christ reconciled us to himself and gave us the ministry of reconciliation; that is, in Christ God was reconciling the world to himself, not counting their trespasses against them, and entrusting to us the message of reconciliation. So we are ambassadors for Christ, God making his appeal through us *(RSV)*.

Strength to Transcend

By faith in Jesus Christ we can find the resources to transcend tragedy. What are those resources that will help us go beyond our problems?

Our basic resource is the gift of the Spirit of Christ, which God gives us. When the Holy Spirit dwells in us, He guides the maturing of our personality so that we can become the people we are meant to be. Jesus Christ, God's Son, is the Mediator between the Father and us—and between us and others. Our relationships then provide the love and caring that others need in order to grow despite suffering in their lives. We can be more authentic in our concern for others when we deepen our relationship with God as a result of our own experiences. What God does for me and with me, He wants to do through me. When I honestly share with others my weaknesses and sufferings and the way God had to work in me, others can gain insight and hope. As one patient said, "If God could help you, maybe He would help me."

Why Do We Care?

One day I was attending to a patient with whom I had worked for two years. Suddenly he looked at me and said, "Why do you care so much for me? No one else has ever cared for me the way you do."

"Because that is the way God cares for me," I replied.

As we become vulnerable to others and actually share the love, peace, and joy that God gives us, they can receive help that is beyond our giving. And an amazing thing happens: We find further healing for ourselves. We no longer need be so concerned about ourselves—our problems, suffering, and needs— but can concentrate on helping others.

After we receive Jesus Christ in our lives, we can converse with God the Father and commune with the Holy Spirit. We were created for that kind of communion. When the Holy Spirit cleanses our hearts and minds, we gain control of ourselves. Then He can begin to manifest himself in our relationship with others.

What we humans need, especially when we hurt, is fellowship with other human beings. Fellowship is not just superficial chatting; it is the in-depth sharing of our whole selves with each other. It is vulnerability, the opening of the inner me to the inner you. It is not a you-talk-and-I-listen session. It is the giving of ourselves to one another without ulterior motives or desires. Through fellowship, we encounter each other as human beings who are part of the same family. We compare our lives—the meanings we find, the problems we have. We come to understand each other in deeper ways.

It works that way for me.

It is not the specific words or answers we give our fellow sufferers, but the sharing of the Spirit of Christ in our relationships with others that makes the difference.

From *Between Faith and Tears*, by Kenneth E. Schemmer, M.D. Thomas Nelson Publishers, © 1981 by Kenneth E. Schemmer. Used by permission.

Chapter 8

Whatever Happened to Integrity?

by Bill Manning

Background Scripture: Matthew 6:19-24; Romans 12:1-2

IT WAS a 10-year-old Chevy van—a church van—and it was in pitiful condition, even for a church van.

• The wheels were so far out of alignment that the van always pulled to the right. But a selling point was that right turns were a cinch.

• The van was equipped with automatic transmission. However, those who drove the van were advised not to get themselves into a situation that required the reverse gear. The drivers were also shown how to crawl under the van and change the transmission to reverse if it did become necessary to back up.

• The van was equipped with factory air conditioning, but the air conditioner wasn't equipped with coolant. On warm days, the van riders were glad that the right passenger window had fallen out. The air flow through the open window was the only air conditioning they had.

• The shocks on the van were shot. So the van rode like a bumper car. Of course, the bright side was that the children enjoyed the bouncy ride.

• Some people who drove the van were distressed that the speedometer did not work. At the same time, the braver souls found driving without a speedometer to be a real adventure.

When the church board reviewed the repairs the van needed, they began to discuss the possibility of selling the van. Apparently, the time had come for them to share this particular one of God's gifts with someone else. The decision was made: They were going to "unload" the bomb on someone. They asked themselves, "How do you get someone to pay to haul off a piece of junk?" Then they came up with some creative ideas to help sell that old wreck of a van.

- It all started when one of the board members agreed to replace the missing window.

- That spurred someone else to say they would take the van to Pete's Paint Palace for the $29.95 paint job.

- Then the pastor suggested it would be good to put some coolant in the air conditioner so that it could produce cool air, at least during the test drives.

- Then a board member who lived on a street with a moonscape of potholes agreed to keep the van at his house while the

"Eight for you, eight for you, eight for—"

church was trying to sell it. That way, all of the test drives would be taken on that bumpy road. A prospective buyer would be less likely to hear the awful engine noise and less inclined to detect that the wheels were out of alignment.

• Before dismissing the meeting, the board members composed the following newspaper ad: "Classic one-owner van for sale. Factory air, automatic transmission, and many other features. Used only to drive back and forth to church."

This board discussion about the church van involved a fair share of good humor. And the more unusual ideas were not used. Yet later, as I reflected on the discussion and on the decisions the board made, it dawned on me that the improvements we had approved for the van were simply cosmetic. The van still had all of its major problems. And the more I thought about it, the more deceptive it seemed we were being.

As it turned out, a board member took the van on as a special project. And it was overhauled from the inside-out. By the time he was finished with it, we were tempted to keep it. So, happily, we survived this situation with our integrity intact.

The kind of deception our board was nearly lured into is the brand that goes on every day. It is all too easy, even for good people, to compromise their principles. I realized that we were dealing with a matter of integrity. I found myself asking: Whatever happened to integrity? And I was reminded of the importance of living in such a way that there is no difference between what we believe and how we live. There should be no difference between our creed and our conduct. Yet in a world where honesty and consistency are almost foreign, there are even Christians who seem to have no idea what integrity means.

St. Paul tells us: "Do not conform any longer to the pattern of this world, but be transformed by the renewing of your mind" (Romans 12:2). J. B. Phillips translates that same verse this way: "Don't let the world around you squeeze you into its own mould, but let God re-make you so that your whole attitude of mind is changed." God wants to help us break out of the world's mold, by remolding us in His image from within. He patiently teaches us to live with integrity.

But what does it mean to live with integrity? At the very least, it means we are to be authentic, undivided, and trustworthy.

Be Authentic

Lee is a real person who has been married for five years. He has a beautiful wife named Jenny, and he loves her. But for several months now, he has been having an affair with a woman in his office. He told his wife he was working late. Recently, the sky fell in for Lee. His girlfriend announced she is pregnant. Lee doesn't know what to do about this unborn child, and he is afraid his sin may cost him his marriage.

Lee must now pay the high price for living without integrity. He compromised his ethics, and now he faces the expensive bill. It is the apostle Paul who tells us "love must be sincere" (Romans 12:9). Those who break out of the world's mold are sincere, authentic, genuine.

Be Undivided

Betty is a woman who is frustrated in her relationship with God. Several years ago she had what she says was a God-given dream to open an elegant restaurant. Everything fell quickly into place except the financing. Betty became fearful that having come so close to realizing her dream, it was all going to slip through her fingers. In desperation, she turned to a financial backer who was anxious to do business with her. However, this backer insisted she alter her plans: He required she serve alcoholic beverages in her restaurant. A bar and wine cellar were added to the floor plans, and Betty was in business. Now, several years later, Betty's restaurant, with its elegant bar, is the picture of success. But Betty will tell you herself she is frustrated and struggling in her relationship to God because of that single decision. She compromised her values. She divided her loyalties. By her own testimony, she will tell you that her success does not make up for the breach of her commitment to God.

The believer cannot display the image of God while remaining in the mold of this world. There is a unity between

God and the believer. This means the believer possesses a unity of heart and mind. It is impossible for anyone to serve God and his own selfish desires at the same time.

People who live with divided loyalties are actually telling God they do not trust Him to work out what is best for their lives. Jesus said: "No one can fully serve two masters. He is bound to hate one and love the other, or be loyal to one and despise the other" (Matthew 6:24, Phillips). St. Paul tells us: "Let us have a genuine hatred for evil and a real devotion to good" (Romans 12:9, Phillips).

Be Trustworthy

Jim and Nancy have been married for four years. They have an active one-year-old boy named Joseph. It was just six months ago that Nancy was injured in a serious auto accident. She still has not recuperated enough to return to work, and the medical bills that have piled up are staggering.

Jim is an auto mechanic. After Nancy's accident, he tried to make ends meet by putting in some overtime hours and by doing some backyard auto work on the side. When that didn't make a dent in the bills, Jim started moonlighting at a nearby convenience store. Before long, between all his jobs, Jim was working 16 hours a day, five days a week. And he would usually put in an additional 12 hours over the weekend working for a custodial service.

This heavy work schedule had begun to take its toll on Jim. He was physically tired, unsatisfied with his work, and frustrated that he could not spend more time with Nancy and Joseph. That's why it seemed like such an answer to prayer when Jim was offered a job at a nearby garage. He had jumped at the opportunity. His starting salary was as much as he made before in the combined jobs, yet he worked about half as many hours.

It seemed like things had never been better for Jim and his family. But then the trouble came. It started after just a few weeks at the new job. The owner of the garage had Jim make a repair with used equipment, but he charged the customer for new parts. And that was only the beginning. Jim noticed it was common practice to make costly repairs that were not necessary. He also learned that customers were being charged for services not performed.

Jim tried to talk to his boss about his concerns, but he was told to mind his own business. Jim found himself in a very difficult place. His salary was good enough that he was just beginning to pay off the family debts. He had felt better physically since he had quit the moonlighting and started working the regular eight to five shift. Still, the best thing about the new job was that Jim had time to spend with his family. On the one hand, Jim had time to spend with his family only because of his new job. On the other hand, the new job required that Jim compromise his values.

It is interesting that Jim decided to quit the new job while he was reflecting on the good times he had been spending with his family. He explained it this way: "To stay at the garage, I had to close my eyes to a lot of dishonest things. And even though it allowed me to spend more time with my family, I didn't want my wife to love that kind of man, and I didn't want my son to have that kind of father."

Here is a man who has broken out of the world's mold. He didn't do what was expedient, or safe, or comfortable, or easy, or self-centered. He did what was right. He proved himself to be responsible and trustworthy.

Those who break out of the world's mold are completely honest. They are trustworthy. Both their words and actions are true.

To walk with integrity is the legacy of God's children. But like any inheritance, it must be claimed. The child of God develops integrity:
- By practicing the presence of God.
- By depending on the power of God's Holy Spirit.
- By keeping at it.

Chapter 9

Stress—a Christian Survival Kit

by Randall E. Davey

Background Scripture: John 16:33; Philippians 4:4-9

Harry was 43 and Becky was 38 when it happened. The three children were all in school that afternoon.

The doctors were pretty frank with Harry. They told him Becky was nearly dead when she reached the emergency room. Seems that old lady Fowler was walking her dog when she heard a car engine running in the couple's closed garage. By the time the police arrived, Becky was unconscious and slumped over the steering wheel. Mrs. Fowler nearly had a heart attack just watching them haul Becky out of the car and onto the stretcher. They said Mrs. Fowler started crying and screaming so much that police threatened to take her to the hospital, too.

When I got to the hospital, Becky was still in the emergency room, lying on a hospital mobile bed, shielded from traffic by a curtain. They had restrained her arms with gauzelike cloth and had given her a sedative. Her droopy eyelids nearly covered a fixed stare. Her dilated pupils focused on nothing in particular, and she seemed to be unaware that I or anyone else was around. For a while she smiled and laughed, and then without apparent cause would cry and clench her fists while whispering undiscernible words.

A psychiatrist was called to talk with Becky, and the doctors told Harry she should be kept for a few days of observation. The kids were really confused, and Harry seemed to be in shock, wandering from Becky's bed to the waiting room and back again, talking primarily to himself and then to Becky. He asked repeatedly, "Why? Why would you do something like that? Why?" Toward evening, Becky quit talking and wouldn't look at Harry. She responded to most questions with a simple yes or no, and when those answers wouldn't work, she just didn't answer.

By the next morning, Becky was irritable, suspicious, and eager to talk. When the psychiatrist entered the private room, Becky raised her head from the pillow and tried to break loose from her restraints as if her ability to communicate was somehow limited by them.

In obvious desperation, she surrendered and started talking rapidly to the doctor, answered questions he had not asked. "I can't handle it. I simply can't handle it." Her words, she remembers today, were deliberate and high pitched. They were final and convincing.

"The kids seem to cry just to aggravate me. My nerves are shot! I've tried for months to keep the house going on Harry's unemployment check. It'll run out in another few weeks. Our house has been on the market since the week the plant closed. So what's new. Everybody's house is on the market around here. Even Harry is acting differently. We never talk anymore, except when friends stop by. Then, it's not really talk. We fall into the same trap, talking about how bad it is in the steel belt. I think he'd leave if he had anywhere to go. He says staying around home is women's work. But I had to go to work just to make ends meet. Harry resents my job, but he knows I have to keep it. We've sold a few things to help out. I cried all last Friday after we sold the old brass bed my grandmother left me in her will."

Her tone softened and her angry expression became more pensive. "Life is so different now. We don't laugh anymore. We don't go anywhere because we can't afford the gas. We never did do much, but more than we do now. A football game, maybe a family night at the roller rink, a ride through the Amish country, and then a carry-out pizza from Papa Johns. Now, no more nights out. No more pizza. I can't believe people's faces when you go to the market. I hate going to the unemployment office. It's worse than a funeral parlor."

For the first time she looked right at the doctor as if he should have some answers. Her demanding look changed, and her conversation became more specific.

"And then today. As if we hadn't had enough, we got a statement from the IRS saying tht we're being audited for three years back. Just our luck. I can't even find my grocery list let alone receipts from that long ago. Instead of feeling like a mother or a wife, I feel more like a survivor, and frankly, I don't have enough energy left to survive much longer. I can't handle it. I simply can't handle it."

They were church people, this family of five. Nothing really unusual about them. Becky was there with the kids every time the church doors opened. Harry usually attended Sunday mornings, coming in a few minutes before worship service started and leaving as soon as the benediction was pronounced.

Becky occasionally joked about being a sports widow, for Harry would faithfully attend the Cleveland Browns home games, and then take every opportunity to march to the woods when hunting season was on. During those fall months, Becky and the children came alone.

In the weeks right before it happened, I would see Becky coming to church, literally dragging her children down the side aisle while their protests could be heard above the rousing opening hymns. On Wednesday nights, she taught the Caravan class for the children. And before she started working, she never missed the Ladies Bible Study. But in recent weeks, she took on a blank stare and sat numbly during the services, when she wasn't fighting with the kids. Really, you could see it coming. She couldn't handle it. She just couldn't handle it.

It was a full six weeks before Becky was released. The doctors gave her condition a fancy name, part of which was in Latin. Translated, it meant Becky could not cope with the stress of the everyday. She felt her only alternative was to end her life. Her release from the hospital was based in part on her agreement to enter into counseling with Harry. At first, he agreed to it, but after a few sessions, Harry concluded that the shrink got his nickname from shrinking Harry's checkbook.

At this writing, Harry and Becky are still together, limping from one crisis to another. Hardly a week goes by that there's not some talk of divorce. Their church affiliation is minimal. Becky told close friends that she was too embarrassed to come back, since the folks knew what had happened. Their future is not a bright one.

Harry and Becky's story represents reality for many of us. One writer has said that *stress* is the catchword of this decade. *Coping, conflict resolution,* and similar buzz words are common ways of describing the way in which our generation is supposed to respond to this unseen but readily felt dynamic of life in the 20th century. The terms are not just found on the lips of executives who guide huge conglomerates. They are just as apt to be spoken by a college student in response to an overwhelming schedule.

More recently, "stress therapists," a specialty in the field of psychology, have edged their way into the seminar market, offering "ways to reduce stress," "how to cope with stress," "how to make stress work for you." Participants are guaranteed ways to "handle" life—a promise that is so appealing to those who "just can't handle it!" These therapists tackle the problem from every conceivable angle, touching on everything from weight loss to time management.

There is also a lot of literature on stress. And most of it tends toward an academic approach, concluding it's a fact of life and ending with a few here's-what-to-do-about-it steps. The general consensus is that stress divides itself into two subdivisions. There is the kind of stress that weaves its way into our consciousness via the news. This is stress from talk about nuclear stockpiles or nuclear winter. Television has given room for numerous talk shows airing the horrendous state of the national and global economy, while other programs show viewers the extent of deprivation and starvation around the world.

Psychiatrists have observed that America is suffering from "nuclear numbing," a term used to describe our inability to feel anger, fear, and rebelliousness that we might if we gave excessive thought to the human predicament. This first subdivision of stressors are ones over which little control, if any, can be exerted.

The second subdivision are those kinds of stressors listed in our case story—very specific, personal situations for which we feel some responsibility (or guilt), and for which remedies are within reach.

It's amazing how popular the "self-help" sections are in any bookstore. Folks still crowd around those new best-sellers, anxious to find a way to eat ice cream every night and still lose two pounds a day. The same holds true for stress-related books. We search in vain to find some secret to maintaining the ever-demanding fast pace of America, but to reduce stress at the same time.

The answers tend to go like this. The first category of stressors, those we can do absolutely nothing about except writing the local congressman and Dear Abby, demands that we adopt a "rain will fall on the just and the unjust" philosophy.

Tomorrow will bring what tomorrow will bring, regardless of what we do or don't do.

Concerning the second kind of stressors, the hints get a bit more practical. Here, a "bull by the horns" approach is taken and the "stressee" is taught how to go into battle daily and emerge unscathed. Here are a few tips:

• **Exercising.** We've heard it for years in response to one ailment or another. It's still just as tough to do once you've started.

• **Eating right.** Once again, it's eat-those-beans-and-carrots time. The idea here is that good nutrition makes us better able to handle the stress that is sure to come. If we can develop a good cardiovascular system, we are more apt to stand the pressure of an IRS audit.

• **Imaging.** This may be a new term, but it's an old idea that works something like this. Your nervous system doesn't know the difference between that which is real and that which isn't. This is why you can wake up in a cold sweat, after you dreamed someone was chasing you. So, trick your nervous system and reduce stress by imagining you are in a favorite vacation site, relaxing in whatever way you please. Doing this a few times a day will give your nervous system a break and thus reduce your stress level.

• **Time management.** Sound familiar? Most of us have seen the little daily calendar and learned to make a list of the most important things we want to get done. Then we lose the calendar. Generally, people who eat up time management techniques simply add more things to their agenda.

• **Thinking positive.** New title to the old book: grin and bear it. Or is it? Perhaps this last standard idea has more possibilities for stress management.

It is rather obvious that stress is common to everyone, in one form or another. Many stressors are well beyond our control, while others come closer to being within our control. Living with stress may be a more viable goal than its elimination. Christian or not, bombs may come. Believer or unbeliever, economies grow strong and then weak. Teetotaler or bartender, the rain does fall on the just and the unjust. But for the believer, the comforter and the Helper is at work.

Consequently, the believer knows:

1. As long as he is in the world, there will be crushing pressure. But One lives in him who has overcome the world (see John 16:33).

2. There are ways of responding to the pressure, stresses, and complexities of life that enable us to support and give support. "Carry each other's burdens" (Galatians 6:2).

3. Good relationship with the Father is through the Son. Daily communion in prayer, augmented by meditation and study of the Scripture, helps us in decision making.

4. Strong family ties are vital. Ephesians 6:1-4 outlines this for us and suggests that a family should operate with sensitivity to each individual member. In our case study, Harry was clearly not the spiritual leader; in a way, he abandoned Becky and the children.

5. Good ties with the Body of Christ are important. Again in Ephesians 6, Paul encourages us to submit to one another. And in Galatians 5 he calls us to serve one another. The resulting bonding builds the Body of Christ and links us one to another so that when one suffers, all suffer, and when one rejoices, all can rejoice.

Exercise will help. Eating properly is good. Vacations in your mind? Well, it's cheaper than the real thing. But when life gets rough and stress mounts to the sky, we can celebrate for we possess a peace that the world doesn't understand. We have a hope that is certain, and, like Paul, we can be content in whatever state we find ourselves.

Chapter 10

When You Lose Your Hope

by Robert H. Schuller

Background Scripture: Isaiah 43:1-3; Jeremiah 17:7-8;
Lamentations 3:22-25

KNUTE ROCKNE SAID IT: "When the going gets tough, the tough get going." When the roads are rough, the tough rise to the occasion. They win. They survive. They come out on top!

People are like potatoes. After potatoes have been harvested they have to be spread out and sorted in order to get the maximum market dollar. They are divided according to the size—big, medium, and small. It is only after the potatoes have been sorted and bagged that they are loaded onto trucks. This is the method that all Idaho potato farmers use—all but one.

One farmer never bothered to sort the potatoes at all. Yet he seemed to be making the most money. A puzzled neighbor finally asked him, "What is your secret?" He said, "It's simple. I just load up the wagon with potatoes and take the roughest road to town. During the eight-mile trip, the little potatoes always fall to the bottom. The medium potatoes land in the middle, while the big potatoes rise to the top." That's not only true of potatoes. It is a law of life. Big potatoes rise to the top on rough roads, and tough people rise to the top in rough times.

Tough times never last, but tough people do.

Judy Hall

In July 1980, Judy Hall, a mother of two young teenage daughters, found herself unemployed. Divorced and without steady income, Judy wondered how she would possibly survive. She had no formal education and no skill that she could call upon.

She was living in Minneapolis, listening to our television program as we urged her week after week to be a possibility thinker. She heard such suggestions as: "Open your mind to God. Ideas will flow in. One of these will be the idea that God means for you to grab hold of."

Judy believed what she heard. So, she decided to try real estate. But she couldn't have picked a worse time to enter the business. As a result, she failed. She could have easily gotten discouraged, but she didn't.

Her next idea was to "take the girls back to their birthplace where they can get acquainted with their heritage." She scraped together enough dollars to pack up herself and her two daughters and return to the state of their birth—Hawaii.

After returning to Hawaii, she wanted the comfort of a muumuu, the loose-fitting dress of the Islands, but also a garment with enough style to be worn to non-Hawaiian events. As she shopped for such a muumuu, she discovered that all of them were sold "off the rack" in one size. All had a similar Hawaiian print, and none really had any distinctive design. And because they were made of the Hawaiian printed fabrics, they really didn't fit any social occasions that were not Hawaiian in tone and spirit.

She suddenly remembered hearing the lesson taught in all

the possibility-thinking literature: "The secret of success is to find a need and fill it." Judy saw a need and decided to fill it. She purchased some fabric in a "mainland" print and proceeded to make for herself a muumuu with a decorative border at the hem. She customized the fit so that it was comfortable but not so loose-fitting as to lose all sense of line and design. The final result was something very distinctive.

Her landlord's wife loved Judy's muumuu.

"Can you make me one?" she asked.

"Of course," Judy said, "I'd love to. When can I take your measurements?"

"Measurements?" she said. "You mean it's tailored to fit me? A muumuu tailored to fit me?" the wife asked.

"Of course," Judy said, "I specialize in custom-made, hand-tailored muumuus. The sleeves should match the length of your arms. The length and the width of the shoulders should be tailored for you."

Beyond a doubt, this was a totally new concept in manufacture and design of muumuus.

As Judy thought about the muumuus she had made, she remembered what we teach in our possibility-thinking lectures: You can test an idea to see if it will be successful by asking four questions.

The first question is: Is it practical and will it fill a vital human need? Judy realized a muumuu is exceptionally practical because it fits any lady, of any shape. Anyone with weight problems can easily hide bulges under the full and flowing style of the muumuu.

The second question: Can it be done beautifully? Judy thought, Yes, the muumuu can have a greater fashion flare. It can be done with more sophisticated draping and tapering and with a layered look like formal dresses on the mainland.

The third question: Can it be done differently enough so that it will stand out from all the others? She decided that it could if she didn't use Hawaiian prints. If she used fabrics that are popular on the mainland, the muumuu would not be restricted to wear at Hawaiian parties.

She asked the fourth question: Can it receive the stamp of excellence and be a little better than anything else that is being offered? Her answer was immediate to the fourth question also. Yes! This muumuu not only would be practical, beautiful, and different but also would excel in value, quality, and style compared to the muumuus currently marketed in Hawaii! With $100 and this confidence she decided to start.

"Dr. Schuller," Judy Hall told me recently, "I made my first muumuu 10 months ago. Today I'm turning out 123 dresses a month!"

"But are you really making money? I know you need to!"

"You bet I am!" she answered.

If a single, divorced mother of two children, with no money and no special training, is able to invade a surplus market with a new product and a new concept and develop a super successful enterprise, then it's probably possible for you to create employment opportunities for yourself.

John Prunty

John Prunty was known throughout his community as "the roadrunner man," for in 1965, running had not become the popular endeavor it is today. There were the usual guffaws and good-natured chiding during his early morning jaunts. On June 6, 1973, John took his usual 21-minute run, not knowing it would be his last.

Later that morning, John, along with the rest of the five-member construction crew, scrambled onto the roof of a small home. It was one of those hot, oppressive days, and the work was difficult. John was atop a scaffold when his foreman called to him for a tool. In reaching for it, John stepped forward, and instantly a cinder block pulled loose and gave way under his weight.

John fought the impulse to jump, thinking that he could regain his balance and avoid breaking an ankle on the uneven turf some 10 feet below. But it was too late. John was already airborne and out of control from his momentum. He seemed to float, as if in a suspended weightless state, similar to flying in outer space.

His flight ended with terrible finality. His 160 pounds landed with full force upon his head, and as John tells it:

"I still shudder when I recall the sickening, grinding sound of crunching vertebrae as they snapped under the strain. My body's trajectory, coupled with its momentum, tried to force my forehead against my chest in pretzel-like fashion. Instantly I was aware I had lost feeling in my legs.

"Waves of fear, anger, and utter frustration assaulted me in those first seconds, as my immediate efforts to get up proved futile. Only my head would respond to my brain's commands. I heard a yell from above: 'Hey, John's fallen!' I alternately cursed and prayed. I turned my head to the left and saw, a few inches away, a pair of booted feet, toes facing me, which looked grotesquely like my own. 'That's strange,' I thought, 'my legs are outstretched!' But they weren't, and the subsequent realization was terrifying.

"I felt no pain until someone lifted my head slightly to place a pillow under it. Then the pain was so severe that I had to request him to remove the pillow. I felt as if my head were suspended only by a thread. Every time I rotated it, even slightly, the pain increased and gave me the weird idea that the thread would break and my head would detach. I struggled to stay conscious.

"At the hospital, the neurosugeon who took my case had me lifted onto an X-ray table. He then climbed up on hands and knees to pull and tug at my head to achieve the needed angles for pictures. Though I had known pain before, I was sure I had never experienced anything like this. A short time later the doctor brought me the unhappy confirmation that my neck was indeed broken, between the fifth and sixth cervical vertabrae. I had learned to pray as a child, so now once again I turned to God and prayed for strength to endure whatever was ahead in life's uncertain road."

During the following weeks, it became more apparent that the major effects of John's injury would be permanent. He continued to hold out hope, though, that a miracle would occur and mend the spinal cord to the extent that it could again process messages—any message—from the brain.

With this in mind, John began to concentrate on recovery. He became interested in discovering as much as possible about just what it was he needed to recover from. He didn't even have to ask, for one day John overheard one of the nurses commenting to an aide, in reference to him, "That's the way quadriplegics are!" John had never before seen a quadriplegic. In fact, he could not spell the word, though suddenly he was one!

In that moment of truth this young husband and father knew he was a quadriplegic, a victim of a broken neck, paralized from the neck down for life!

But he was alive! It was a tough time.

He said, "I decided to be a survivor. In fact, three D's became my guiding theme ... desire, dedication, and determination. I knew I needed to generate and sustain the *desire* to live, to heal, and to recognize my true potential. Then I had to *dedicate* myself to that concept. *Determination* alone would give me the victory. I resolved never to surrender!"

Today, John claims that life is every bit as good as ever.

He says, "I know there is no place in my life for recrimination, bitterness, or hate. I feverently believe that to hate is to destroy.

"I decided my accident was something I could never escape from. It would become a millstone around my neck, or if I practiced possibility thinking, I could turn my millstone into a milestone! I decided to do just that! I have accepted *me* as I *am* rather than as I *wish* I were. I need but to smile or wink at a wide-eyed child in the supermarket, as I buzz down the aisles in my electric wheelchair, to elicit a comment like one youngster made recently: 'Gosh, you're lucky!' "

John does more than wink or smile at children. Today he manages his own business, serving surrounding hotels and his community with a professional baby-sitter placement service. He also gives many hours as a volunteer counselor in the New Hope crisis telephone counseling center in the Crystal Cathedral. Because of the new hope he has found, he is able to give new hope to the discouraged people he counsels.

Carol Schuller

In the four-year period of 1978-82 we watched our daughter, Carol, move from a hospital bed to the ski slopes.

When we arrived from Korea to Carol's bedside in Sioux City, Iowa, after her motorcycle accident, I was shocked. She lay in her bed in intensive care. Her body was bruised, broken, and disfigured. But her spirits were whole and healthy.

On the long trip back from Korea, I had searched for my opening line. What would my first words to her be? She solved the problem by speaking first: "I know why it happened, Dad. God wants to use me to help others who have been hurt."

It was this spirit, this positive attitude, that carried her through seven months of hospitalization, intravenous feedings, and consequent collapsed veins. This positive attitude gave her the courage to fight a raging infection that threatened her left leg as well as her life. She hung on until a new drug was released by the FDA. It was the right drug at the right time—a real miracle.

It was that same positive attitude that helped Carol make the transition from hospital patient to a "handicapped" member of a family and school. It helped her feel normal and whole again.

She refused to allow the inconvenience of an artificial leg to keep her from pursuing the active life she loved, including softball.

She has had six surgeries since that first amputation. Today she is skiing and has met her goal, which was to win a gold medal in the qualifying races that, in turn, admitted her to that elite corps of skiers participating in the National Ski Championships! In March 1983, she pulled her goggles on and took her place among the champions in the country—at the young age of 18 years! Yes, she still walks with a limp. She draws curious looks from strangers. But her positive attitude helps her even with that.

A few summers ago my family and I were privileged to be the guests of the American-Hawaiian Steamship Company on a one-week cruise of the Hawaiian Islands. It was absolutely beautiful! On this cruise, it is customary on the last night to have a talent show in which any of the passengers can participate. Carol, then 17 years old, surprised us one day by saying, "I'm going to be in the talent show tonight."

Now Carol doesn't sing, and of course she doesn't dance. So, naturally, I was curious as to what she would do that night. Carol is not the least ashamed to be seen in shorts or swimming attire, although her present articifical left leg covers her stump to just below the hip. But she is very conscious of the fact that people look at her out of corners of their eyes and wonder what happened to her.

On Friday evening, the night of the talent show, my wife and I sat in the lounge along with 600 other people. The talent show was scheduled to take place on the stage in the big, glorified cocktail lounge. As you can imagine, it's a very secular scene. The acts that were performed that night were typical of amateur talent shows. Then it was Carol's turn.

She came on stage wearing neither shorts nor Hawaiian garb, but a full-length dress. She looked beautiful. She walked up to the microphone and said, "I really don't know what my talent is, but I thought this would be a good chance for me to give what I think I owe you all, and that is an explanation. I know you've been looking at me all week, wondering about my fake leg. I thought I should tell you what happened. I was in a motorcycle accident. I almost died, but they kept giving me blood, and my pulse came back. They amputated my leg below the knee and later they amputated through the knee. I spent seven months in the hospital—seven months with intravenous antibiotics to fight infection."

She paused a moment, and then continued, "If I've one talent, it is this: I can tell you that during that time my faith became very real to me."

Suddenly a hush swept over the lounge. The waitresses stopped serving drinks. The glasses stopped tinkling. Every eye was focused on this tall 17-year-old blonde.

She said, "I look at you girls who walk without a limp, and I wish I could walk that way. I can't, but this is what I've learned, and I want to leave it with you: It's not how you walk that counts, but who walks with you and who you walk with."

At that point she paused and said, "I'd like to sing a song about my friend, my Lord." And she sang,

> *And He walks with me,*
> *And He walks with me*
> *And He tells me I am His own,*
> *And the joy we share*
> *In our time of prayer*
> [originally, "as we tarry there"]
> *None other has ever known.* *

"Thank you."

There was not a dry eye, not a life that wasn't touched that night. *Tough times never last, but tough people always do!* Because tough people know that with men it may appear impossible, but with God *all things are possible!*

Chapter 11

When Someone You Care About Does You Wrong

by David Augsburger

Background Scripture: Matthew 7:1-5; 1 Corinthians 13:5-7

I NEVER LIKED THAT CAR—we shouldn't have bought it in the first place," your wife tells you. You're standing in the kitchen holding the crumpled chrome strip you just pulled loose from the smashed fender of your Corvette.

"Why didn't you tell me you scraped the side of the car?" you say low—and with overcontrolled tones.

"It's just the fender. I scratched it."

"Scratched it? Who did you hit? Did you get a ticket? Does he have insurance?"

"Slow down. It was nothing like that. I scraped a post coming out of the parking lot. No accident. No police. No problem."

"Except for our $100 deductible insurance. Where were you looking?"

"Straight ahead. We shouldn't have bought that car to begin with. You paid too much for it. You had to have it. Thought it was sharper looking than Bill's, so you paid through the nose . . ."

"Cut it out!" you bellow. "That's got nothing to do with this fender." You toss the chrome strip onto her white tablecloth. "We're talking about you trying to move a concrete abutment with a Corvette."

"You should be happy I wasn't hurt," she says. "If I had been run over by a truck, you'd come stomping into the hospital and throw a greasy fender on my bed."

"Oh, for crying out loud, stick to the problem will you?"

"That is the problem," she says. "The problem is us. Not a piece of metal."

"The problem is I've got to pay for a smashed fender."

Nothing ends blaming games like the recognition that the blame must be scored 50-50.

Nothing settles old scores like the recognition that everything finally comes out even. That's how it is in any ongoing relationship. If there is blame to be fixed, it includes both persons involved.

It takes two people to have a problem. In a marriage, for example, neither I nor you is the whole problem. "We" are our problems. The trouble is with "us."

Both people are involved in the hurt, the problem, the tragedy of a marriage in pain.

Blame is 50-50. In marriage, both people deserve each other. All tends to come out even in the end.

Example one: "He's the problem," the wife says. "I've given him the best 20 years of my life. I've cared for him in sickness and in health; I've borne him three children; I've never refused him anything. Now look. He betrays me with some little tramp. See how I was wronged?"

Good speech. Good case for scoring blame 90-10. Ninety for him—the villain; 10 for her—the virtuous wife. Agreed?

Highly unlikely. When you've heard them both, things even out. Once you see how righteous and superior she appears to him, the score comes nearer 50-50 again.

Example two: "It's all her fault that our son ran away," a husband says. "She nagged at him mercilessly. She criticized his choice of friends. She picked at his hair, his clothes, his way of speaking. She refused to accept the girl he was dating. So the boy left. She drove him away."

He makes a good case for scoring the tragedy 99-1. Ninety-nine points against her, one for his own responsibility.

But when you've heard both sides it evens out. In this case, the dad kept his distance from his wife since the boy was quite young. His cool withdrawal taught the boy how to reject and write his mother off. So the boy did in reality what his dad has been doing all along—withdrawing, rejecting, running away from relationship and intimacy.

"Trading for this car was your stupid idea," your wife says angrily. "Now we're stuck with the lemon."

"That's not true. We bought the one you wanted."

"We were taken. It's your fault."

You hit the starter one more time. It turns over but doesn't grab.

"You've been had," she says.

You give the ignition key another angry twist. If only it were her ear. She talks you into the car, then blames you for buying it. Or did you buy the one she liked knowing you could blame her when something goes wrong? Either way, you're both being had in these no-win battles. Somebody's got to make a move for honesty.

"Jill," you say, "we're getting farther apart every time we fight. You're out to win by putting me down. I'm out to win by putting you down. We both lose. I don't care who wins. I just want to be close to you."

There's surprise all over her face.

"That's what I really want, too," she says.

Whose fault is it when things go wrong? That's the first question that arises in many human difficult moments. For those who prefer placing responsibility elsewhere, the question leads to a wild-goat chase for someone who can be scapegoated with the main load of blame. For those who prefer to sponge up the anger and store it away inside, the blame can be taken heroically upon themselves. "It's all my fault," they say, "I'm the total failure." And even more people do both. At one moment they blame themselves for the whole tragedy, at the next they take another swing at the scapegoat.

Blaming ourselves is useless, for a variety of reasons.

We usually blame ourselves for all the wrong reasons. (The crucial things that went wrong are not likely to occur to us alone.)

We're not qualified to sit in final judgment of our own lives. We so easily slip into either total rejection, "I'm no good at all, I don't deserve to live," or we excuse ourselves lightly, "So what, I'm only human." (To assume the right to sit in judgment over my motives, my past, and my true condition, is to play God.)

I don't truly understand my past. I know that my memories are selective. I recall those things that fit with my self-image.

Friedrich Neitzsche, the German philosopher, put this pointedly, saying, "Pride and memory had an argument. Memory said, 'It happened thus and so!' Pride replied, 'Oh, but it couldn't have been like that!' and memory gave in."

So it is for us all. Memory gives in again and again. Most of the pictures we recall from our past have been retouched. Most of the scripts we can quote from old conversations have been edited for us by pride.

Memory is a museum.

Room on room of memories are instantly available as one flashes through collections of choice recollections at will. Musing through your museum, note how selective the artifacts are. Are they art or fact? Did you create them to meet your needs or capture them to record reality?

Memory is mystery.

"I can see it now exactly as it happened," you may insist. But it isn't true. The best you can do is produce a biased series of fragments that serve to reassure you that things were as you wish they were. Or they may warn you to be sure they do not recur. The truth of your past is known only in part. Even to you. Especially to you.

Memory is a myth.

Some people believe that memory is a camera. They assume past events are accurately recorded through an objective lens and preserved unretouched. We have no objective past. Our reflections are just that. My memories mirror me and my needs, my values, my dreams, my interpretation of my serial life experiencs. Memory is not a telescope for looking at a sharply etched and permanent image. Memory is a kaleidoscope that reviews the past, rearranges its detail, reinterprets its meanings for the challenges of the moment. My story is my mythology of my life that guides the organization of my life. Memory is a compass that may repaint the scenes recalled but still points toward integrity. Memory is a gyroscope that balances the self and maintains harmony and unity within.

Memory is my story.

Myth or mystery, it's still my story, and a story worth telling. Yes, it has been thoroughly edited by my pride. Memory reports what took place and pride rewrites the data before the conscience—the perfect scribe—can get at it. Yes, it has been recycled and the most recent forms may be made up of the original atoms, but the anatomy has matured. Still, it's my story of who I am today, what I am becoming now, where I stand in this moment.

"Museum tours daily, 9-5."

Venture into your museum. Claim the rooms. The treasure is yours. Explore. The valuables are precious property. They are evidence that you have lived, risked, failed, learned from the pain, grown, celebrated, broken free.

There are a few rules in the museum.

Appreciate the collected objects of art. Don't abuse the privilege of visiting your past. Do not vandalize your valuables. Look at them in appropriate awe. Do not criticize them. Prize them.

Respect the recollected experiences. Use them for you, not against you. Learn from them how to choose more freely, how to live more fully, how to act more faithfully in the future.

Acquit the memories from any and all charges. To attempt to change the unchangeable is useless. What is done is done.

Be humble enough to take pride in your past. Great or small, it's yours. Have the grace to be grateful for having lived. Accept the grace to own how you have lived. Absorb the grace that frees you to delight in what you have lived.

Going through our old memories to place blame is like hunting for a black bead in a dark room at midnight wearing heavy gloves and a blindfold.

I want to, rather simply, own my past with as few defenses as possible, and live now in the present before God and with my brothers and sisters.

Recognizing how unable I am to judge myself brings me to awareness of how unqualified I am to judge a sister or a brother. Since my vision is as impaired as though a beam of wood were protruding from my eye, I am poorly equipped to remove splinters from others, as Jesus put it unforgettably.

Pass no judgement,
and you will not be judged.
For as you judge others,
so you will yourselves be judged,
and whatever measure you deal out to others
will be dealt back to you.
Why do you look at the speck of sawdust in your brother's eye,
with never a thought for the great plank in your own?
Or how can you say to your brother,
"Let me take the speck out of your eye,"
When all the time there is that plank in your own?
You hypocrite!

First take the plank out of your own eye,
And then you will see clearly
To take the speck out of your brother's.
(Matthew 7:1-5, NEB)

Paul put it:

Love keeps no score of wrongs;
does not gloat over other men's sins,
but delights in the truth.
There is nothing love cannot face;
there is no limit to its faith, its hope, and its endurance.
(1 Corinthians 13:5-7, NEB)

Love ends the blaming games and gets on to the real questions: What is the loving, responsible, truly respectful thing to do now? Where do we go from here? When do we start? If not from here—where? If not now—when? Who—if not you and me?

Loving is owning responsibility, breaking the lead from the fine-line bookkeeping pencil, tearing up the scorecard, and beginning again. *Now.*

From *Caring Enough to Confront,* by David Augsburger. Published by Herald Press, © 1980 by David Augsburger. Used by permission.

Chapter 12

Coping with Old Age—
Yours and Your Parents'

by Nina Beegle

Background Scripture: Psalm 71:9, 18; Ecclesiastes 12:1-8; Isaiah 46:4

MERCILESSLY the mirror stared back at me, startling me with its duplication. Clearly my skin didn't fit so well anymore. And the tributary lines on my forehead . . . oh my! . . . It was too late for Oil of Olay. If only I had left my glasses on the bedside table, as I usually did upon waking. But there I was in living color, and mirrors don't lie. I had to say it:

"Mirror, mirror on the wall.
I really don't feel that old at all."

The Birth of Aging

Aging begins when we are born and ends when we are either snatched away unexpectedly or our bodies grow old and say, "Enough. I quit." The realities of aging must be faced, and each of us will determine if this is done with calm acceptance or bitter regret. But I never heard anyone say he was anticipating it. We look forward to it because we have to. Perhaps that look-in-the-mirror is everyone's first awakening to the onset of Demon Age, with his bagful of bulges, bunions, and bifocals.

Gail Sheehy in *Passages* said, "To be confronted for the first time with the arithmetic of life was, quite simply, terrifying."

A dear friend of mine in her mid-50s put it more succinctly. She shocked me one day with, "Getting old is hell!" It seems to me that such a natural process ought never to cause such disquietude, particularly for those who put their trust in the eternal God. The Lord's securities extend to the end of life and

"Sort of like turning back the mileage on a car, isn't it?"

beyond: "Even to your old age and gray hairs I am he, I am he who will sustain you. I have made you and I will carry you; I will sustain you and I will rescue you" (Isaiah 46:4).

What foreboding force was kicking up the silt in my friend's psyche? Perhaps the fear and stress came because she was reluctant to let go of the things of the world or because of the loss of youth, which the world venerates; or beauty, which the world worships; or status, which the world respects; or position, which the world honors. None of these values is eternal, however, and it would seem the Christian should be equipped to get the reality of aging into perspective.

The Scary Part of Aging

Still, some dread and fear are bound to gnaw at the edges of the most sanctified philosophy of aging. The scary part is not so much that youthful beauty has vanished and left in its place a mottled serenity, but that there are so many "what-ifs." Is that what the Psalmist was feeling when he said, "Do not cast me away when I am old" (Psalm 71:9)? Perhaps that is the worst fear of all—"What if I become a castoff?"

Pat Moore, who wrote "Journey into Old Age" for *Guideposts,* experienced those feelings. She was only 26 when she disguised herself as an elderly lady. With wig, simulated wrinkles, and cane, she placed herself in situations that often confront older people, especially as they require or need help. That she was a pretty girl, no doubt accustomed to preferential treatment, made the rejection she experienced from her experiment even more poignant. The elderly are no longer venerated as in Bible times. Even 30 years go it was unthinkable to leave an elderly person standing in the bus aisle while a younger person sat; now, to rise and give a seat to an older person would be conspicuous. But God has not removed His decree: "Rise in the presence of the aged, show respect for the elderly and revere your God" (Leviticus 19:32).

And so it is that today's society treats the aged as useless. But that is progress in reverse. Time and experience, says the adage, are the greatest teachers. Why do we not see the logic? The worst kind of stewardship is that which relegates the pensioner to a rocking chair. You don't have to be up to riding a pogo stick to be productive in the church and the community.

Most of the Old Testament characters experienced their greatest achievements on the down side of "the hill." Caleb was in his 80s when he said, "I'm just as vigorous to go out to battle now as I was then" (Joshua 14:11). He went out to claim a mountain: "Give me this mountain" (v. 12, KJV) and he did it because he "followed the Lord . . . fully" (v. 8, NASB).

Moses, his forerunner, was in his 80s also, when he delivered the Israelites from Egypt.

Abraham was 99 years old when the Lord said to him, "I will confirm my covenant between me and you and will greatly increase your numbers (Genesis 17:2). Abraham was "very fruitful" in the ensuing years and became the "father of many nations" (Genesis 17:5).

Gideon was an old man when he subdued Midian, then lived to see the Israelites enjoy 40 years of peace.

In a more contemporary vein, consider Art Stone of Sandy Spring, Md., who at 87 owns and operates six sawmills. "I can do the work of two men," says Art, who gets up at 5 A.M. every day and does a full day's work. Stone is an artisan whose work can be seen in such places as the White House and luxurious Georgetown estates in Washington, D.C.

We all have heard about Grandma Moses. But did you know that her painting career began when she was 78, and it continued for many years?

We need our older people—to help us keep our perspective, to pray us through the thick of spiritual battle, to help us nurture the younger generation in the church, to counsel the young marrieds. The church should be especially sensitive to employing their wisdom and experience.

In the community, pensioners can foster Bible studies, do volunteer work in hospitals, nursing homes, and halfway houses, and give refuge to "latch-key" children who get home from school before their parents get home from work. The opportunities for meaningful service are endless once we escape the eight-to-five treadmill.

Perhaps even more at the downside, life should be viewed as something to give, not as something to get. However, if productivity is to grow with the progression of age, it will not happen because we suddenly thought about it. Somewhere between rocking horse and rocking chair we must set some goals for ourselves—spiritually, mentally, and physically.

William S. Deal in *Maturing Gracefully* says, "All you will be in old age you are now slowly becoming . . . Old age is not blocked off as a section of life or separate pasture into which one is automatically turned out to graze at retirement age. It is simply the extension of his normal life into the range of a longer time of life!"

Deal gives simple, practical advice on preparing for old age. And it adds up to the biblical injunction to do all things moderately. A healthy diet, exercise, and sleep, in proper doses and beginning at age 20, will inevitably affect the quality of life at age 60.

Likewise, our mentality is set in concrete by attitudes and thinking patterns we develop. "The maturing process itself," says Deal, "has nothing in it that should add to life bitterness, discontentment, resentment, ill will, frustrations, hostility, and many of the other traits older people often manifest. These

94

things are not the results of aging but the leftovers of a failure somewhere in earlier life to make the correct adjustments to life and maintain the right attitudes deep down in the subconsciousness." He suggests that if we don't entertain bitterness or animosity, and if we do learn to laugh at ourselves and find solutions to our problems as we come to them, we will mature gracefully.

It is impossible to put an evaluation on early beginnings as they affect our spiritual development. To have lived a life for Christ is to approach old age, even death, with a serenity of spirit that baffles the world. It certainly takes the fear out of the what-ifs to know God is in control of one's life.

Planning Ahead

Just as health, mental attitudes, and spiritual outlook are affected by planning and application, so may our financial welfare be benefited. Real financial security is something we may never have, and even when we think we have it, the future is about as dependable as a weather report.

Arthur A. Hyde, a president's cabinet member of some years back, said, "I never knew but one man who had economic security, and he didn't want it. He was a 'lifer' in a federal penitentiary."

Nevertheless, we can and should do everything possible to ensure independence for our later years. None of us wants to be a burden on our children or society.

No matter how well you've planned financially, you are going to feel much better prepared to leave this world if you have made some simple preparations for leaving. It is not morbid, for example, for a couple to make early arrangements for their burial and funeral. But leave your funeral arrangements open to change. Your family will appreciate it.

Pre-death plans prepared by funeral and mortuary entrepreneurs should be investigated thoroughly. Look for the plan that insures you and your spouse so that any unpaid balance is written off at the time either of you dies. Be sure your cost for burial place, coffin, vault, and other provisions included, are locked in at your purchase price—not subject to inflation. Most plans do not charge interest and can be paid off at the rate you choose.

Don't expect the mortuary entrepreneurs to volunteer information that will cut your expenses. Ask! Cremation, for example, allows the customary funeral, but from that point on cuts the cost of dying considerably. There are other shortcuts you can discover by writing to the American Association of Retired Persons. You will want to discuss with your family any drastic measures, such as donating your body to medical science (which erases all burial expenses).

It is not expensive to have a legal will drawn up, and that is a *must,* whether you are 25 or 85. It will keep your estate, however small, from falling into probate. Even your furniture, your books, and the pictures on your walls need to be designated to someone. Many a family has become estranged over a piece of antique furniture.

Your first phone call regarding the drawing up of your will could be to the religious denomination with which you are affiliated. Many give free service to their members. Accommodating them in your will is a courtesy and a privilege you may want to exercise in return for this service.

Don't overlook the possibility of donating one or more body organs as your last contribution to life on earth. You might want to talk it over with your children and include this in your will. Also, for their sakes and your own, you may want to make a statement releasing them and your doctor from the responsibility of decision in the event a long mechanically induced existence on life-support systems becomes an option.

Undoubtedly, the best preparation in life or in death is to have treasures laid up in heaven, but if we can also lay up a few on earth it can help those we leave behind.

Who's to Care for the Elderly?

To Vera, who sits all day slobbering in a wheelchair and who gives the nurses her pitiful, toothless grin when she finally makes clear her garbled request, positive thinking is just so much mush. And Henry, in the hospital with cancer snaking its slow, tortuous way through his body—to him, old age IS a living hell on earth. The pain is real. The shame is real. The portent of financial disaster is frighteningly real. Do we say to these, "Be ye warmed and blessed"?

Perhaps the worst of all is the loss of privacy. Vincent thinks so. A former county clerk and judge, Vince was an outgoing, gregarious guy with a crazy sense of humor. He pursued many things and was active in politics and church until, at 65, diabetes began its destructive pursuit. Cataracts removed from both eyes left him barely able to read, attacking the very core of his life. Recently, at age 78, Vince's leg was amputated. Now he's confined to a nursing home. He's learning, or is supposed to be, how to maneuver in a wheelchair. It's extremely difficult for him because two strokes have left his remaining limbs very weak. His wife has broken her hip and can't be with him. Vince wants to go home and deal with his situation in the privacy of his home. But he has no control over his life anymore.

Vince's pastor has made one call in the last five months. Seldom does anyone from the church ever come. Vince is lonely and depressed. What scriptures shall we quote to him?

Perhaps that question could be answered with another: What else is there to offer Vince, or Henry, or Vera that will help? Their only hope is in Christ, in the comfort of His Word. But the Word is more powerful when it has hands and feet. Prayer will help—but with hands and feet. Much of the pain of old age has to be in the loneliness that comes from being forsaken by friends, family, and society. Everyone else seems so busy with the very stuff of life that the languishing older folk wish they could be a part of.

Alice's family tried to help. They took her in because she was getting unable to care for herself and was so forgetful they feared for her safety. But one day she heard them talking about how hard it was to have her there, so she decided to go live with her sister down South. Her sister would be glad to have her, she knew. But her sister was dead; she had forgotten that, too. She managed to pack some things and get to the bus depot. Standing in the ticket window, she couldn't answer the agent's question, "Where to?" She couldn't remember where her sister had lived. Her family found her sitting in the bus depot in despair, crying and confused. As much as they hated the idea, they knew they had to put her in a care facility. The happy ending to the story is that Alice felt secure there and much happier because she had people she could relate to and things to occupy her time. For her, living with the younger members of her family was not the right answer.

So what is the right answer? No answer is right for every situation or every family. Each family must find its own best answer.

When My In-laws Moved In

In our case, the decision to take both my husband's parents into our home, right or wrong, was very costly. In two different nursing homes, they pled to be removed. They had raised nine children and, in their minds, it was reasonable to assume that one of the families could take them in and care for them.

We were no more able to take on such a responsibility than the other brothers and sisters, but we drove 350 miles to see if their complaints were valid. At lunchtime, we watched as Papa's tray came with cold soup and fluffy white bread soaked with instant orange juice that had slopped over. The shared-bath situation was difficult for Mama because of her particular illnesses. There were other things.

Their son, my husband, felt a biblical responsibility for their welfare, since no one else had volunteered to help them.

In the middle of their first night in our house, a thud set the ceiling to vibrating above our bed. A wail followed. My husband and I leaped from bed and raced up the stairs. With a 12-inch advantage over me, my husband was the first to reach the shaken heap on the bedroom floor. It was Mama. She had fallen out of bed.

Nightly interruptions became regular. Papa's pad-padding above us meant that he was wandering around again, confused. But he could remember the telephone numbers of his children and would call them and tell them he needed help and no one was taking care of him. Another night he fell and broke his hip. I dashed up the stairs to find that his fall had landed him up against the little space heater we provided because they were never warm enough. A fire was barely averted. That was when we had him put back into a nursing home. I think he felt we were punishing him. It broke our hearts, but he needed the care they could give him. He didn't live long after that. I doubt he felt there was a whole lot to live for.

In this arrangement, the first injustice to our children came when we had to push Becky out of her bedroom (the first time she'd ever enjoyed the luxury of having her own) because it was the only one with a private bath. We sectioned off, with bookcases, one end of the recreation room for her. No closet.

The second injustice was that our extra time and energy were almost totally occupied in trying to satisfy the wants and needs of two sick, elderly people who had all day to concentrate on how they felt. The doctor had prescribed for each a total of 18 pills a day, which helped neither their ability for sound reasoning nor their dispositions.

The interruption of our total life-style was shattering to the children. We couldn't attend functions together with them. One of us had to stay with Mama and Papa. That was the case even for our own daughter's wedding. In hurt and rebellion, our children turned away from us, to more available but less desirable mentors and compatriots. My husband and I were bone weary every night, and the only quality time we seemed to find for the children was when they came into our bedroom and we all plopped ourselves on the big bed and talked in undertones. The living room was off limits. Since we could not afford to furnish Mama and Papa's bedroom as living quarters, the living room was where Mama parked and surveyed our family goings-on from behind her serving tray with its load of liquids, tissues, disposal bag, and other non-goodies.

Finally, our teenage daughter married unwisely, partly (we have since learned) to get away from the situation at home, and partly to get her own place since she was pushed out of her rightful place in our home. Tragedy that would fill a book visited that marriage and our daughter's life.

And so we learned the hard way that it is not always best to take into the home elderly parents. Sometimes it's best for everyone if you seek out a quality care facility for the elderly parents you love.

It's a tough decision to make. But sometimes, it's the most Christian decision you can come to.

Getting On with Life

Today I sat on a small pier jutting into Indiana's Lake Chapman. As I gazed into a baby blue sky, I exulted in the call of a mourning dove, the splash of a beaver, and the rhapsody of a dozen birds happying-up the atmosphere. I felt immersed in the ceaseless ecology of life. I was exhilarated by the magnanimity of God that enamated from His creation to me. My sense of awareness and delight have not diminished since I passed the half-century mark; I am more perceptive of life's pleasures and processes than ever before. I am more grateful. I drink of life more fully.

Friendships and associations are enjoyed more deeply.

Love has more depth and glows more brightly.

With the anxieties of youth gone, even sex is more enjoyable.

Assuming we have maintained reasonable health and freedom from dire financial straits, past-50 can be spent at the end of a rainbow. We are better equipped to enjoy life than ever before, and most of us are no longer trying desperately to prove something. We are able to snuggle down into the ongoing processes of life. We are free from what Carroll Freeman calls in *The Senior Adult Years,* "the desire that tempts us with illusion"—about more money, better jobs, fancier cars, or in general, beating out the Joneses. "Within us something more powerful is stirring. We experience in the quiet hour that we are part and parcel of God's creative plan, not 'then' but now."

Sheehy describes past-50 tranquillity this way: "People who have seen, felt, and incorporated their private truths during midlife passage no longer expect the impossible dream nor do they have to protect an inflexible position . . . A great deal of behavioral red tape can be cut through once people have developed judgment enriched by both inner and outer experience."

Though speed may decline in the elderly, test performance shows that accuracy seldom does. We can go back to college "just for the fun of it" or take a trip to Spain because we always wanted to see the inside of an old castle, or write a book because now we have the uninterrupted time.

Shall we get on with it?

Chapter 13

Death: The Longest Good-bye

by Becky Smith

Background Scripture: Ecclesiastes 3:1-4; 1 Corinthians 15:21-22, 51-57

GLANCING NERVOUSLY at the clock, I realize that it is past time for Greg to be coming home from the lake. Today is such a beautiful day for fishing; perhaps he is just stealing a few extra minutes to enjoy his favorite pastime. Peeking through the curtains of my kitchen window, I marvel at the flaming reds, intense yellows, and brilliant oranges mingling with dying browns as autumn splashes her glory on the western North Carolina mountains.

With the sun beaming down in the crisp air, laziness and peace prevail. Maybe the day's mood has made time unimportant to my 12-year-old Huck Finn. He is always so dependable. I'm sure he'll be along any minute. Lately he has grown so much that his daddy even lets him take the boat out alone. It still makes me nervous, but Sonny says, "Trust him, Mama. He's growing up."

I know his daddy has taught him well, for the happiest times of their lives have been spent on the lake whiling away precious hours becoming friends. Catching fish is only an excuse. Occasionally they allow Tonya, our eight-year-old daughter, and me to join them if we pledge not to talk too much and scare away the fish. Oh, the happy times we have shared as a family!

Beautiful memories of such sweetness and love engulf me as I hungrily search the road for the sight of Greg's rich auburn hair glistening in the sun. Where can he be? He should be hurrying along now with his fishing pole slung over one shoulder, fish strung on a stick, and Fonzie, his dog, trotting devotedly behind. Anxious thoughts flood me. "Hurry home, honey," I whisper.

Suddenly a familiar pain rips through me, gouging my insides. He's not coming home! Not now! Not ever again! He's dead! He's dead! My son is dead! A scream tears my throat. Choking it back, I beg, "Oh God, please help me. My beloved little redhead is gone. I can't touch him or see the freckles dance on his face again. I can't hear the joy of his laughter. I won't ever be able to watch him grow again. Why, God, did his precious life have to end so tragically before he even had a chance to live?" The scream claws for release.

Running to the living room, I fling open the draperies and anxiously look for Sonny. He is my rock, my strength. I have to hang on until he gets here. He'll hold me and soothe the pain. "Sonny, where are you? Don't you know I need you? Greg is dead. The pain is unbearable. You've always taken care of me and I need you now! Hurry!" Carefully I listen for the engine's

whine and the creaking of the camper cover as his truck hits the rain holes in our dirt drive. "Oh, God, please hurry. I can't hold on much longer!"

Suddenly realization explodes within me. As I crumble to the floor, sobs rack my body. Sonny won't be coming home! Not now! Not ever again! He, too, is dead! dead! dead! Both of my men ripped from life in the seconds it takes an airplane to drop from the sky. Why, God, why? The scream tears again with pain so intensely real that I quiver with convulsions. I have to hold on. If I let go, I'll fly into a million pieces!

Holding on has been the name of the game for me since this nightmare engulfed my life. The horrors of that day are burned forever in my soul. What started out to be a delayed Christmas holiday for the Floyd Smith family in Florida ended in tragedy so real and devastating that the effects are still vibrating in the lives of us all.

On December 26, my brother-in-law, Jack Smith; his wife, Floy; and their 26-year-old son, Richard, flew from Arlington, Tex., in their new single-engine airplane while we drove from North Carolina. Joining the families of another brother and sister, we feasted on turkey and dressing with all the trimmings and topped off the meal with homemade pumpkin pie—all lovingly prepared by Grandmother Smith to welcome her family home. The house rang with the laughter of children, grandchildren, and even a great-grandchild as we exchanged gifts and renewed the bonds of love which tied us together. Brimming with plans for our time together, we retired at peace with the world.

The next day dawned so crisp and clear that Jack, Richard, Sonny, and Greg decided to take a pleasure ride in the plane. The girls wanted to catch the after-Christmas sales, so we casually kissed good-bye, unaware that death lurked at our doorstep. When the plane began circling over the house a short time later, Granddaddy Smith sauntered into the yard to wave. Sweeping low, they snapped his picture and began soaring off into the distance. Granddaddy was 77, and his steps were slow as he turned toward the house. Suddenly he froze as an ear-splitting crash thundered through the air. Quickly he scanned the sky. The airplane had disappeared! Catching sight of a crumpled mass of metal in the open field, he began hurrying toward it. Inside lay our four men—all dead! Time stopped for them at exactly 2:10.

I can't describe the shock, numbness, disbelief, denial, and devastating turmoil that erupted that day. An emotional roller coaster was set in motion that has been whirling madly ever since. I can't get off nor can I slow it down. In those brief seconds, my world was shattered. I didn't think I could go on living, and frankly I didn't even want to. All at once I had become a widow, a single parent, head of a household, and breadwinner. I became Tonya's only security. I was brutally thrust into a world where decisions had to be made, and I alone had to accept the consequences. I became an object of pity, a frightened figure enfolded in arms of love by an entire community—a love that has helped me through days when I felt I couldn't go on. I became a person with strengths I didn't know I had. On that day, in those seconds, death began leading me down a grief-filled trail, making me face and cope with situations I believed impossible. Death began forcing me to grow in new directions.

The first and harshest reality I raced was death itself. *Death.* What an ugly, frightened world! For most people my age—34—death has little or no meaning. It's something that happens to old people in the natural scheme of things. For me, it now means pain, real physical and emotional pain plus rivers of tears. It means an aching to touch Sonny's face, kiss his lips, or hear his voice. It means an empty bed and whispers of love ringing silently through a lonely night. It's hearing the haunting strains of a saxophone playing "Danny Boy," his favorite song. It's missing his accepting love and yearning for shared secrets with my best friend. It means screaming in the night when dreams of blood and twisted metal torture the sleep. It means thoughts of suicide that creep slyly in and play havoc with frayed nerves as they offer the comfort of an escape from pain.

Death means going to church and seeing two caskets flash before my eyes and images of 110 high school band members dressed in full uniform at rigid attention with tearstreaked faces watching the bodies of their director and his son carried into the church. It's seeing pain as they lovingly place roses on the caskets. It's standing before 950 weeping students in assembly and presenting the Marion O. Smith Memorial Music Award while choking on tears, every nerve in me fighting the reality of saying good-bye to the students of East Henderson High School.

Death means weeping for a son whose life was just beginning. It's missing the excitement of his giggles about girls or his pride at winning the student council election for second vice president of the student body. It means wandering into his room alone and holding the rabbit skin he called his good-luck charm or his blue ribbon for the school's best leaf collection. Seeing the trumpet he was beginning to play in his daddy's band makes me shudder. Death means crying alone in his room at night. Because only a mother knows the miracle of childbirth, no one else loves as a mother loves. And no one mourns as a mother mourns.

Yes, death is a reality I've had to live with. Ours is a death-denying society, but we all have to face it sometime. There is no preparation for it and no defense against it. It will come and only the Christian, one who has accepted Christ, has hope.

In the months following the accident, death forced me to even painfully question that hope and reexamine faith. There have been times when I've wanted to lash out at God. How could He let this awful thing happen? Once last fall while watching the remnants of Sonny's band perform, I cried out, "Oh, God, I hate You for what You've done to our lives!" Instantly I recoiled in horror. What had I said? Then slowly I realized that even though I said I did not blame God for the crash, I still held Him responsible. He could have prevented it. Why would He allow such a tragedy? The lives of all four of the dead men were so full of meaning and so rich in potential for service. They were fine Christians, active in their churches and communities. How could He let them die? I tried so hard not to be bitter, but unanswered questions kept gnawing away at me.

Jack and Richard were a close father and son and were

leaders of our church's Scout group. Jack founded the troop, and for 25 years he had shaped the lives of young men through scouting. Just before Christmas he had turned the leadership over to Richard, who was full of plans for continuing and enriching the activities. Now their usefulness was gone. They were dead.

Sonny's work in our community was reflected in the lives of hundreds of students through his 10 years of teaching music, his contribution as cofounder of the Hendersonville Summertime Band, his assistance to many local church music programs, and his service as president of the Western Carolina Bandmasters Association. He was closer to his students than a regular classroom teacher because he started them in the seventh grade music program and kept them through graduation. Greg, Tonya, and I were so wrapped up in his band work that his students literally became part of our family, a relationship we loved. Sonny did not talk religion; he lived it. He taught by example. When he said, "No smoking and no drinking," it was because he did neither. He expected his students to meet high standards and rarely was he disappointed. Before each performance, the band would have a moment of silence and then pray together. It was a special time and one we all grew to cherish.

Greg's death has made me cry out most often to God against the injustice of it all. Only 12 years old, he never had a chance in life! The image of his father, he was developing the same delightful sense of humor, the same sensitivity to other people, the same appreciation of human dignity. From the day he was born, he brought us joy and delight. I could see in him so much potential for a purposeful life. How could God let him die? How?

I've searched for answers and found none. I've begged people to tell me why. I've prayed for understanding. I've probed my faith and questioned God. I've cried until I can't cry. Slowly I've come to the realization that God did not cause the accident. He allowed it to happen and when death came, He lovingly accepted them. On faith, I've begun to believe that from this tragedy, God will work His purpose. I still don't understand, but as a friend lovingly pointed out, God is supreme. He is in control. He knows best, and, therefore, I must believe and rest.

With a deepening sensitivity, I have reexamined cherished values and struggled to a new understanding of life as we live it daily. Death has made me restructure my priorities. The Serenity Prayer, "O God, give us serenity to accept what cannot be changed, courage to change what should be changed, and wisdom to distinguish the one from the other," has given me courage for this.

I cannot change the death of Sonny and Greg. All the tears in the world won't bring them back. I must change myself and adjust to changed circumstances or life will overwhelm me. I've been torn by conflict, saddled with unwanted and unwelcomed responsibilities, tossed by an emotional storm until I've begged for relief, cried until seemingly there could be no more tears, and hurt until I don't want to hurt anymore—but I've held on! I've kept the scream stifled inside me, and I've continued my job of teaching school and tried to maintain a normal life for Tonya.

We've continued to live in the same house, see the same friends, go to the same church, and do the same things. We've survived birthdays, anniversaries, and holidays. We talk. Sometimes we laugh about the good times. Sometimes we just cling to each other and cry. But steadily we have grown. Steadily we have learned to refuse tomorrow's problems today. And steadily, with God's help and guidance, we are learning to live just one day at a time.

From *Home Life*, January 1980. Copyright 1979 The Sunday School Board of the Southern Baptist Convention. All rights reserved. Used by permission.